THE POSTURES OF THE ASSEMBLY DURING THE EUCHARISTIC PRAYER

JOHN K. LEONARD AND NATHAN D. MITCHELL
with an introduction by John F. Baldovin

A project of the
Notre Dame Center for Pastoral Liturgy

LITURGY TRAINING PUBLICATIONS

ACKNOWLEDGMENTS

Liturgy Training Publications gratefully acknowledges the Notre Dame Center for Pastoral Liturgy, University of Notre Dame, for providing us the opportunity to publish this manuscript.

The cover photograph is of an 11th century fresco of St. Clement and others at Mass. © Collegio San Clemente, Via Labicana 95, 00184 Rome.

This book was edited by David A. Lysik. The production editor was Deborah Bogaert. It was designed by Kerry Perlmutter, typeset by Jim Mellody-Pizzato in Trajan and Trump Mediaeval, and printed by Versa Press, Inc.

Library of Congress Cataloging-in-Publication Data
     Leonard, John K.
The postures of the assembly during the Eucharistic prayer / John K. Leonard, and Nathan D. Mitchell ; with an introduction by John F. Baldovin.
     p.   cm.
     "A project of the Notre Dame Center for Pastoral Liturgy." Includes bibliographical references and index.
     ISBN 0-929650-64-6 : $11.95
     1. Posture in worship. 2. Eucharistic prayers — Catholic Church. 3. Catholic Church — Liturgy. I. Mitchell, Nathan. II. Title.
     BV197.P65L46   1994
     264'.02036—dc20   94-31581
                                           CIP

CONTENTS

PREFACE

> A common posture, observed by all, is a sign of the unity of the assembly and its sense of community. It both expresses and fosters the inner spirit and purpose of those who take part in it.

With these words, the *General Instruction of the Roman Missal* begins its description of the actions and postures of the eucharistic assembly. This book is an examination of this principle as it pertains specifically to the postures assumed by the assembly during the eucharistic prayer.

The book is divided into four parts. Chapter One offers a Christian view of what may be termed the anthropological roots of posture and gesture. Because of the indissoluble unity of the human person as "body/soul," corporeal gestures are capable of bearing transcendent significance— they are not merely educative or instrumental, they are "doors to the transcendent" that actually open us to the presence and impact of Mystery. Bodily gestures do not merely "describe an attitude"; they enact the relationship described by that attitude.

By an examination of posture in the Graeco-Roman, biblical and liturgical traditions, Chapter Two considers the many sociological and religious attitudes enacted by standing, prostrating and kneeling. It will be shown that any posture can express several different relationships simultaneously, while a particular emphasis or focus is determined by the ritual context.

Chapter Three considers posture at ritual meals during the time of Jesus and the early church. Although the celebration of the eucharist was eventually separated from the communal meal, the sociological and theological significance of the meal continued to have implications for the way the eucharist was understood and celebrated throughout the first millennium. Its relevance for the renewal of Christian life and worship in our time should be obvious.

The final chapter traces the evolution of posture during the eucharistic prayer, from the patristic era to contemporary praxis in North America.

The history and the theology of the tradition speak for themselves. Those who read this book are free to draw their own conclusions.

An Embodied Eucharistic Prayer

by John F. Baldovin, SJ

THE BODY AND LITURGY

The great contemporary choreographer Martha Graham was once asked by a group of journalists, after a premiere, what the meaning was of a particular dance she had performed. She responded: "If I could have told you what it meant, darlings, I wouldn't have had to dance it."

Graham's response is far more than a witty turn-of-phrase. It says something profound about the nature of symbolic gesture and, by that token, ritual. In other words, if it were possible to express ourselves and our understanding of the world around us merely by logically connected statements that could be set down in books, then we would have little or no need of symbol, gesture, art—or liturgy. Robert Hovda made the same point eloquently when he wrote about the importance of vesting liturgical ministers:

> Like so many sense experiences that rationalist types dismiss as trivial, liturgical vesture has a considerable impact on the feelings of the assembly as a whole as well as on those exercising a particular role of leadership.
>
> Anyone who, contrary to the most elementary human experience, persists in the stubborn conviction that ideas, points, arguments are the stuff that move human beings, is natively unfit for liturgical leadership, if not for liturgical life.[1]

Hovda was reacting to what might be called the rationalism of the post–Vatican II reform of Roman Catholic liturgy. The enormous and valuable success of the reform was to teach us that the word of God is supremely important in worship. It has a kind of pride of place as the first part of every liturgical celebration; it governs (or should govern) our preaching; it inspires every sacramental action. But clearly, however, the word of God alone is not sufficient for Catholic worship

1

because it needs to be enacted. The gospel, after all, consists of the teachings of Jesus, his actions, and the surrender of his whole self.

Now, while the restoration of the liturgy of the word to pride of place, and the expansion of the lectionary and indeed the new appreciation for reading and understanding the Bible all represented a tremendous breakthrough for modern Catholicism, these things also coincided with a certain tendency toward rationalizing Catholic worship and piety. After all, one could discover in the prophets of Israel, in the gospels themselves, and especially in St. Paul, that external actions without interior dispositions are vain and empty—in fact a kind of mockery of God.[2] Furthermore, God cannot be confined to particular times and particular spaces; genuine worship takes place in spirit and truth (John 4).

This attitude fits perfectly with a culture that increasingly scrutinizes psychological motivations and interior dispositions and respects the sovereign freedom of the individual. In addition, all of these attitudes are healthy and point to important recoveries of fundamental aspects of Christian faith. But, at the same time, when they become the exclusive focus of communal worship so that all external actions are called into question, they make truly communal worship anemic. In short, it is simply naive to imagine that *only* interior dispositions count or to think that any religious group can do without communal actions that embody their beliefs in ways that reasoned discourse cannot accomplish.

Perhaps a minor but not insignificant example will be helpful. At the announcement of the gospel reading during a eucharistic liturgy, the priest or deacon makes a sign of the cross on the gospel book or lectionary and then signs himself on the forehead, lips and heart. The people, while responding "Glory to you, Lord," also sign themselves. The meaning of the gesture is fairly straightforward: We want the gospel to inform everything we think, say or do. The gesture connotes a connection between an external action (signing oneself with the cross) and an interior disposition. One can only guess at the motivations for omitting this gesture. Perhaps it seems awkward; perhaps it smacks too much of ritualism (ritual as empty show or neurotic preoccupation); perhaps people simply dislike participating in an action that has never been explained; perhaps such minor omissions cater to a kind of adolescent need to rebel, to claim one's individual identity. Of course omitting this gesture is not the end of the world, but it does betray some disregard for what could be called the *communal choreography* of liturgy.

One of the (many) functions that rituals (and therefore liturgy) perform is to help a group of people experience solidarity, identity and common purpose. And the very reason they need ritual is to express that identity *bodily* and *communally*. My point here is not to persuade people to sign themselves with the cross at the liturgical proclamation of the gospel so much as it is to argue that what we do communally with our bodies at worship makes a great deal of difference when it comes to one of the main reasons for public worship in the first place—namely, to express who we are as a community in the presence of the living God.

It is not for no reason that the Orthodox have been characterized as "the church standing," the Roman Catholics as "the church kneeling" and the Protestants as "the church sitting."[3] These basic bodily postures communicate a great deal about the self-identity of these Christian communions. Though none of these postures is exclusive to the church that it characterizes, each one tells us something about basic attitudes: standing as praising God with upright bodies, kneeling as an act either of adoration or of penitence, and sitting as an act of receptivity, listening and participating in a common meal. Each posture certainly has its advantages, and each makes a great deal of difference in the self-understanding of the church.

In order to consider the issues involved in the posture of the assembly during the eucharistic prayer, perhaps at this point it will be helpful to discuss the multilayered meanings of the sacrament of the eucharist. Please note that what follows, as well as the historical essay by John Leonard and Nathan Mitchell, is not so much an attempt to convince Christian communities to change their posture during the eucharistic prayer as it is an attempt to analyze what is at issue in this question of posture.

THE ASSEMBLY AT THE EUCHARIST

The eucharist is such a rich symbol of the Christian faith that it resists any simple explanation. As a ritual symbol (i.e. a symbol in action), it has been treated by theologians and preachers in various ways: as the presence of the Lord, as a representation of the sacrifice of Christ, as a communion meal, as a banquet that looks forward to God's eschatological reign, as the communion of the body of Christ, Head and members, as a source for the forgiveness of sins and the healing of illness, or as an effective means of praying for the dead.[4] As the central ritual expressing Christian faith, the eucharist has attracted all of these meanings for some two thousand years. At certain times, one or several meanings might be emphasized at the expense of others. The task of the church is to discern which of the many meanings might stand out today without losing the others.

In the reform of the liturgy that was sanctioned by the Second Vatican Council, the participatory and communal nature of the liturgy was underlined in an effort to encourage contemporary Catholics to become more actively engaged in their faith—both within the walls of the church and in their daily lives. The key to this shift in the understanding of active participation in the liturgy can be found in the *Constitution on the Sacred Liturgy*, which insists that such participation is the right of the faithful by virtue of their baptism.[5] Furthermore, by the recovery of the adult catechumenate through the *Rite of Christian Initiation of Adults*, we can recover another root meaning of the eucharist that lay dormant for many centuries—that is, that the eucharist is the ongoing, repeated culmination of Christian initiation. This meaning remains clouded for the church today by the practice of having confirmation follow first communion for those baptized as infants. But the clear witness of the early church shows that eucharist as *incorporation* into Christ serves as the culminating moment.

We are very slow at realizing the importance of this sequence of integral initiation (baptism, confirmation, eucharist) because it suggests such a profound change in piety and spirituality.[6] The sequence of baptism, first confession, first eucharist, then confirmation emphasizes the connection between penance and the eucharist, whereas we might rather emphasize the intimate connection between baptism and the eucharist—a relationship in which confirmation serves as a kind of hinge whereby the assembly publicly recognizes what has been accomplished in baptism so that the newly baptized might enter fully into Christ.[7] A recovery of what could be called "baptismal dignity" thus lies at the basis of the current reform's understanding of liturgical participation. It also leads to a richer understanding of the eucharist, one in which the members of the assembly celebrate not only the memorial of what God has done for them in Christ but also how this has concretely been part of their own experience of being made into Christ through initiation. This approach respects both the individual and corporate dimensions of liturgy and reveals liturgy for what it is—the corporate and ritual expression of the whole of Christian life, with its goal as incorporation into Christ. Because this is never a "finished product" this side of the eschaton, the eucharist enables us to grow into this incorporation throughout our lives.

Specifically how the eucharist enables us to be incorporated into Christ remains to be discussed. Over the centuries, there have been any number of attempts to explain precisely how the person of Christ and his sacrificial activity on behalf of humankind are present in the eucharist. Many of these explanations centered on either the presence of Christ in the consecrated bread and wine or on the representation of Christ's sacrifice because (unfortunately), from the beginnings of scholastic theology, these two questions have usually been treated separately. In fact, questions of sacramental theology became disconnected from commentary on the liturgy, and the latter tended to take the form of an allegorical exposition of the life, passion, death and resurrection of the Lord.[8]

In addition, the baptismal focus discussed above took a back seat to questions about the role of the priest in the celebration of the eucharist.[9] One might be able to arrive at a better explanation if the focus were shifted from the priest to the whole of the assembly celebrating the eucharist corporately. Such an explanation would have to integrate the notions of real presence and sacrifice, not to mention other important aspects of the eucharist such as thanksgiving, meal and invocation of the Holy Spirit.

The place to begin such an explanation (or at least give a sketch) is with the structure of the liturgy itself.[10] Is there something about the ritual structure that reveals the meaning of the eucharist and leaves room for other significant aspects of eucharistic theology and piety? And is this basic structure discernible? The answer to both questions is "yes," and that answer is based on what Gregory Dix called the "shape of the liturgy." Dix discerned a relatively universal shape for the eucharistic liturgy, based on the actions of Jesus as recounted in the narratives of institution found in the New Testament.[11] Dix claimed that the seven actions that Jesus performed at the Last Supper (taking the bread, blessing it, breaking it and giving it at the beginning of the meal, and taking, blessing and giving the cup at the meal's end) were from the very beginning collapsed into a four-fold action (taking, blessing, breaking and giving) in the church's eucharistic practice. While it is not possible to argue either that this move was immediate or universal or that such a uniform shape to the eucharist was likely, given the diversity of the earliest Christian communities, Dix's basic insight holds true for the vast majority of evidence up to the Reformation of the sixteenth century. At this time, a number of churches "juggled" the pattern in an effort to recapture the literal sequence of the New Testament institution narratives—for example, by having the consecrated bread distributed immediately after the words "This is my Body." But one can also find a weakness in Dix's theory in that he underlines the meaning of "taking" as offertory without adequate basis in the tradition, reading back into the church's early practice from the medieval Roman rite.[12]

But it is still true that the basic structure of the eucharist can be discerned: The church "takes" the bread and wine in the presentation of the gifts, "blesses" God in the eucharistic prayer, "breaks" the bread in the fraction rite and "gives" it in holy communion. It is crucial to note here that these are the actions of the church rather than of the priest alone. Though the priest may play an essential role in the articulation of the Church's blessing and thanking God, the whole of the eucharistic action is fundamentally corporate because the whole of the assembly is both invited to the act of communion and represented in the other three actions by its ministers.[13]

Further, if the eucharist, like any sacrament, is the act of Christ (head and members), it is reasonable to argue that the rite itself somehow reveals who Christ is. Now, the Last Supper acts in the gospels as a kind of acted parable. Of what? In general, of who Christ is, and specifically, of his passion, death and resurrection—the paschal mystery. It is, as Dix called it, a "dress rehearsal for the Passion."[14] Why is the church's eucharist an apt ritual symbol of this paschal mystery? Because the church does precisely what Christ did—it offers itself (with Christ as its head and in the power of the Holy Spirit) to the Father in free and loving obedience so that true life (the life of God) might be shared. It cannot do this without accepting that life in the first place and allowing itself to be broken. So the four-fold action of the eucharist becomes a means of expressing Christ's self-sacrificial offering and, *at the same time,* is a ritual expression of the life of the church (as individuals and community) as members of his Body. The death to sin and evil that is effected in baptism is operative again and again in this ritual form so that the structure might shape us into what we already are (though in process)—the Body of Christ.[15]

If this sketch of the shape of the eucharist and how it might form the basis of an adequate eucharistic theology is on target, then a number of conclusions follow. First, it would be a mistake to focus on the role of the priest and neglect the ritual role of the assembly as a whole. This is not simply sloganeering or banner-waving egalitarianism that wants to level the (necessary) distinctions of role and status in a church that is hierarchically structured; rather, it is an attempt to understand the role of the priest as a minister of Christ precisely because he is a minister of the church. Second, this sketch enables us to integrate the real presence of Christ with his sacrifice, in the context of his (the church's) prayer of thanksgiving and invocation of the Spirit and in the context of the sacred meal as a communal anticipation of the heavenly banquet. Third, it affirms the closest possible connection between the church's eucharist and Christ himself, Christian initiation and daily Christian living. Fourth, by stressing the ritual act itself, it avoids any number of church-dividing questions like the "moment" of consecration. Fifth, it places the eucharistic prayer in proper perspective as the articulation of the whole of the shape of the eucharist, which reaches its culmination in the corporate act of communion.

Though this section has merely sketched out a possible approach to the structure of the eucharist and the theological meaning that may be derived from it, it may help us to sort out some of the implications for posture during the eucharistic prayer.

THE POSTURE OF THE ASSEMBLY

As we have already noted, the ritual of the eucharist has supported a variety of meanings throughout the centuries; but a particular meaning or set of meanings might predominate, given historical and social circumstances. For example, communion of the faithful has always been a meaning of the eucharist. It became much less important, however, in the centuries when the unworthiness of the faithful and the mystery and awe attached to God's activity in the eucharist were emphasized. It is but a short step from this insight to perceiving the links between posture at the eucharist and the meanings that predominate; in other words, the basic shape of the liturgy might remain the same while the meanings attached to it or to parts of it shift. This can be true not only historically but also across cultures—and it is no less true of the era of the Tridentine Missal, during which the language and the rite may have remained the same but the eucharist took on varied nuances depending on the culture in which it was celebrated. "The Mass is the same wherever you go" may have been true for the pre–Vatican II traveller from the United States, but that was the case because he or she could attach a familiar meaning to it and need not have attended to the cultural meaning involved. Of course, this is not as easy to do today because of differences in language.

In their essay, Leonard and Mitchell show that the earliest posture of the members of the assembly that we know of is standing with arms upraised (usually called "the *orans* position"). Kneeling was introduced as a gesture of adoration combined with supplication in the course of the Middle Ages, when full participation gave way to devotional attendance and controversies arose regarding the real presence of the Lord in the eucharistic elements. Further, they show that according to rubrics, people were only expected to kneel at low Mass rather than at solemn or sung Mass. The post–Vatican II reform of the liturgy shifted the emphasis from bare-bones celebrations to the Sunday sung eucharistic celebration that seems to have become normative in practice as well as in theory. On the other hand, kneeling became the required posture at all eucharistic liturgies—at least from after the Sanctus until the end of the memorial prayer *(anamnesis)* that follows the institution narrative. Such a solution need not cause us too much puzzlement when we recognize that so much of Vatican II and the subsequent reform has consisted of a determined effort to blend the old with the new.

When asking the question about the posture of the assembly at the eucharist, we must be very careful to locate it within as rich an understanding of the eucharistic liturgy as is possible in our circumstances. Therefore, the question of kneeling or standing (or sitting for that matter) should be coupled with a theological understanding of the eucharist as a whole.

The question may be asked within the context of a theological understanding of the eucharist that emphasizes the communal nature of the rite, as a representation of the pattern of the Last Supper, which allows us to enter into the mystery of the Lord's passion, death and resurrection. If such an understanding governs our eucharistic practice, then it would seem to make sense for the entire assembly to remain standing throughout the whole eucharistic prayer, not just during the preface, as is the current practice in the United States.

If, on the other hand, our theological understanding is focused on the activity of the priest acting in the person of Christ, then a somewhat more passive posture of kneeling during the eucharistic prayer seems warranted as a physical means to encourage adoration of the Lord present in the consecrated bread and wine.

That the former posture corresponds better to the practice of the early church is not in itself a persuasive argument; church practice develops in response to the needs of the times. But the contemporary recovery of liturgical participation based on baptismal status, and a shifting understanding of the role of ordained ministry in the church, might well warrant considering a change in posture that corresponds more closely to a communal model of the shape of the eucharist.

But what of adoration and reverence? Are these values to be discarded simply because they seem less important than a new sense of active participation in the liturgy? In other words, is merely standing during the eucharistic prayer sufficient to communicate participation in this sacred act of thanksgiving that articulates the church's faith and transforms the simple gifts of bread and wine, in the power of the

Spirit, into the life of the world? The real question to ask here is: How will standing be embodied *as prayer?*

The simplest solution might be for the members of the assembly to raise their hands in the traditional *orans* position. This form of participation lasted until at least the ninth century, as one can see in the miniature of the *Drogo Sacramentary,* in which the faithful with open hands are standing and bowing during the eucharistic prayer. It is a posture with many advantages, since it connotes praise, supplication and vulnerability. Of course it requires that the members of the assembly be holding nothing in their hands. Another possible posture would be to stand with hands folded in the more modern gesture of prayer.

This approach is not meant to create prejudice against kneeling at the liturgy—for example at the penitential rite, the litany of the saints or the exposition of the blessed sacrament. The question, rather, has to do with whether kneeling is appropriate at the eucharistic prayer.

Moreover, if the members of the assembly were to stand during the eucharistic prayer, they might well be invited to a more "choreographed" participation, for example by bowing as the priest bows or genuflects. One of the mistakes made at the time of the introduction of communion in the hand was a failure to provide adequate instruction on how this might be done reverently—a mistake difficult to recoup after people had started receiving in whatever way they saw fit. Now there is far too little choreography in the contemporary Roman Rite, on the part of both the people and the ministers. For example, the somewhat elaborate gestures of the priest, like bowing and then signing himself with the cross at "may be filled with every heavenly blessing," were never adapted for the people in all of the eucharistic prayers. It would be a pity if standing during the eucharistic prayer were introduced without giving people the means to make this a reverent act of prayer.

CONCLUSION

In this essay we have focused on the intimate connection between the body and liturgical piety and theology. At a time when people with contrasting pieties are often members of the same assembly, there are no simple solutions to the question of posture during the eucharistic prayer. At the very least, however, we must be attentive, both to how our theology and piety will shape our postures and gestures in the liturgy as well as (perhaps even more to the point) to how bodily attitudes at worship will shape our theology and piety. What we do with our bodies at worship has far more effect on our experience than we usually think. The question before the church today is not *whether* our liturgical prayer will be embodied, but *how*.

ENDNOTES

1. Robert Hovda, "The Vesting of Liturgical Ministers," *Worship* 54 (1980): 112.

2. See, for example, Isaiah 1:12 –17; Amos 5:21–24; Matthew 15:7–9; 1 Corinthians 11:17–22.

3. See Burkhard Neunheuser, "Les gestes de la prière à genoux et de la génuflexion dans les églises de rite romain," in *Gestes et Paroles dans les Diverses Familles Liturgiques*, Conferences Saint-Serge (Rome: Centro Liturgico Vincenziano, 1978), 153.

4. For the many-layered meaning of eucharist, see the convergence document of the World Council of Churches' Faith and Order Commission, *Baptism, Eucharist and Ministry* (Geneva, 1982). This product of multilateral ecumenical dialogue describes five main meanings of the eucharist: thanksgiving to the Father, memorial of Christ, invocation of the Holy Spirit, communion of the faithful and meal of the kingdom. The statement is also known as the Lima Document. See also the lyric catalogue of the many occasions for which the eucharist has been celebrated in Gregory Dix, *The Shape of the Liturgy* (London: Dacre Press, 1945), 744.

5. Vatican II, *Constitution on the Sacred Liturgy (Sacrosanctum Concilium)*, no. 14.

6. For a wonderful and imaginative exposition of "integral initiation" in the early Church, see Aidan Kavanagh, "A Rite of Passage," in Gabe Huck, *The Three Days*, rev. ed. (Chicago: Liturgy Training Publications, 1992), 171–175.

7. For further explanation of the roots of confirmation, see Aidan Kavanagh, *Confirmation* (Collegeville: Pueblo, 1988), 39–78.

8. See Josef Jungmann, *Missarum Sollemnia: The Mass of the Roman Rite*, I (New York: Benziger, 1951), 113–116.

9. See, for example, David Power, *The Sacrifice We Offer: The Tridentine Dogma and Its Reinterpretation* (New York: Crossroad, 1987), 172–176.

10. Here I am very sympathetic to the treatment of "pattern" as advocated by Gordon Lathrop, *Holy Things: A Liturgical Theology* (Minneapolis: Fortress, 1993), 33–36, and to the notion of "ordo" that he derives from Alexander Schmemann, *Introduction to Liturgical Theology*, 2nd ed. (Crestwood, NY: St. Vladimir's Seminary Press), 28–39. Unfortunately Lathrop (p. 47) has some difficulty with Dix's parsing of the shape into four actions and insists that prayer and communion form one action. I agree with him on a theological level that the rite is one, but Dix's discernment of four actions still seems valid.

11. I am using the term "relatively" here because there are celebrations, like that described in *Didache* 9–10, that do not fit his scheme. But, though Dix can be faulted on any number of individual judgements in *The Shape of the Liturgy*, his basic thesis that the shape reveals the meaning of the liturgy still holds true in my opinion.

12. See Robert F. Taft, "Toward the Origins of the Offertory Procession in the Syro-Byzantine East," *Orientalia Christiana Periodica* 36 (1970): 73–107.

13. That is the whole of the assembly in the persons of those who are in a right relationship with God and who are adequately prepared.

14. Dix, *Shape*, 77.

15. No doubt this theory will seem to some to come dangerously close to allegorization. I suppose I must plead guilty but point out at the same time that allegory had the virtue of wanting to tie the liturgy as closely as possible to Christ.

CHAPTER ONE OUTLINE

I. The indissoluble unity of body and spirit

II. The significance of postures in the liturgical assembly

THE ANTHROPOLOGY OF POSTURE AND GESTURE: A CHRISTIAN VIEW | 1

THE INDISSOLUBLE UNITY OF BODY AND SPIRIT

Body and spirit belong essentially to the definition of the human person. Both the Hebrew and the Christian Scriptures avoid anthropological dualism and affirm the original *unity* of persons as both *"flesh"* (body) and *"spirit"* (soul, breath of life). The Bible, generally, does not think of the human body as something "external" to the human "I," as something that the "I" possesses as a mere tool, as an instrument or agent for its actions. Rather, the body is something that human beings *"are."*[1]

THE SIGNIFICANCE OF POSTURES IN THE LITURGICAL ASSEMBLY

The indissoluble unity of flesh and spirit in Christian anthropology is the fundamental basis for understanding the significance of postures in the liturgical assembly. Just as the body is the real "symbol" of the soul, so physical gestures are the real symbols of those attitudes that flow from a human being's soul. Only by being expressed in bodily gestures do those attitudes truly *come into being and*

15

acquire existential depth.[2] To put it briefly, *gestures are the real symbols of spiritual attitudes and intentions.* Gestures incarnate intentions—and in the very act of incarnating them, those spiritual realities begin to exist. They actually come into being, truly expressing and embodying themselves. As Joerg Splett has written (in non-gender-inclusive language):

> [M]an is as a whole and essentially a bodily entity. He has a body and at the same time he is his body in a true sense. He can never distinguish himself adequately from his body. On the contrary, he is the particular man he is precisely on account of his body (individuation). So too the upsurge of his enthusiasm in work and love does not lift him above and out of his body, nor is death simply the separation of body and soul. In his body, man is opened out to his environment and the exterior world becomes accessible, attackable . . . and vulnerable; his body disturbs and hinders his development. But it is in the body and its activity that man shows himself and sees himself: There, the "invisible soul" becomes visible (art of self-expression). In the body, man "knows" man (Genesis 4:1—sexuality), and man comes to be by means of this fully human event (generation). In the body he is bound up with and allied to the sub-human—he is "dust" (needs, instinct); but in the body (as in itself something spiritual, and not merely because his spirit is in it) he is also higher than the sub-human. The body is man's "primordial activity" (G. Diewerth), the "symbolic reality" of man (K. Rahner), his "medium of being" (B. Welte), in which he lives and "is there" and is present—precisely insofar as it is not the body itself that is intended (e.g., pleasure, the voice) but the essence and its reality (love, the song).[3]

With this Christian anthropological understanding, it is possible to make the following observations regarding gestures, postures and movement in the liturgy: Because of the indissoluble unity of the human person as "body/soul," corporeal gestures are capable of bearing transcendent significance. Bodily gestures are thus not merely educative or instrumental; they are "doors to the transcendent" that actually open us to the presence and impact of Mystery. Bodily gestures do not merely "describe an attitude"; *they enact the relationship described by that attitude.* Dropping to one's knees enacts adoration, supplication, contrition or repentance—it does not simply "describe" these things or "educate" us in their desirability or significance.

Hence there exists the "weight" classically attributed to ritual gesture and bodily action in the sacraments. No one has expressed this more concisely than Tertullian († c. 220):

The flesh is the hinge on which salvation depends. As a result, when the soul is dedicated to God, it is the flesh that actually makes it capable of such dedication. For surely the flesh is washed, that the soul may be cleansed; the flesh is anointed, that the soul may be consecrated; the flesh is sealed, that the soul too may be fortified; the flesh is shadowed by the imposition of hands, that the soul too may be illumined by the Spirit; the flesh feeds on the body and blood of Christ, that the soul as well may fatten on God. What is united in service [viz., flesh and spirit] cannot be separated in destiny.[4]

ENDNOTES

1. From the perspective of scripture, it is more accurate to say we "are" our bodies rather than that we "have" bodies. "Flesh" and "body" are biblical expressions for the *whole* person understood in the historical conditions of physical freedom and constraint, strength and weakness, power and vulnerability. Similarly, "soul" and "spirit" designate the *whole* person by denoting the human capacities for self-reflexive awareness, for entering into relationships with others, for forming bonds with the absolute mystery of God through acts of self-transcendence.

2. On this point see K. Rahner and H. Vorgrimler, *Theological Dictionary*, C. Ernst, ed., R. Strachan, tr. (Herder & Herder, 1965), s.v. "Symbol."

3. In K. Rahner, ed., *Encyclopedia of Theology* (New York: Seabury, 1975), 160.

4. Tertullian, *De Resurrectione Mortuorum*, VIII.2–3; *Corpus Christianorum, Series Latina* [CCL] II: 931. Translation from Paul Palmer, *Sacraments and Worship* (London: Darton, Longman & Todd, 1957).

CHAPTER TWO OUTLINE

I. Standing

A. The anthropology of standing

B. Standing for prayer in the Bible

C. Standing for prayer in the church

D. Summary

II. Prostration and Kneeling

A. In the Greco-Roman world
   1. Adoration as an act of kissing
      a. Adoration as action
      b. Kneeling or kissing the feet
   2. Adoration as an act of prostration or kneeling
   3. Conclusions

B. Scriptural and early Christian examples of the use of *proskynein* and its synonyms in various ritual contexts

C. Kneeling for prayer in the liturgy
   1. Sacramentaries
   2. *Ordines Romani* and Pontificals

D. Kneeling as veneration and adoration
   1. Veneration of the cross
   2. Summary

E. Honor of persons

F. Kneeling: worship of the eucharist

The Sociological and Religious Significance of Standing and Kneeling | 2

P atterns of posture and gesture, especially in the context of eating and drinking, "describe" relations of social distance (of intimacy and proximity). It is still the case in every instance of human eating and drinking that differences in roles are recognized by differences in posture.[1]

As we shall see, any particular gesture or posture can have many different, even contradictory, meanings; postures and gestures always have to be interpreted from within their contexts. But even then, there may be many layers of meaning present in any particular gesture.

STANDING

THE ANTHROPOLOGY OF STANDING. Standing erect on two legs was precisely one of the characteristics that in the course of evolution helped distinguish *homo sapiens* from the rest of the animal world. There is, then, something distinctively human about this posture. At the same time, the human ability to stand erect on two legs (as the normal posture used for work, conducting business, greeting one another, etc.) reminds us that, once upon a time, we "betrayed" our animal origins. The human posture of bipedal standing—insofar as it represents self-conscious choice—points to the line crossed when we first entered the realm of self-awareness; it is an ability that forever would distinguish us from our earlier animal ancestors.

Thus on the one hand, standing represents primordial human arrogance—the unshakable conviction that we are superior to the rest of creation as well as our uncritical assumption that the world was made for our service, use and pleasure. Contemporary theologies of creation and new understandings of the relationship between religion and ecology now challenge this. Standing is the posture of self-confidence, of human "sovereignty" over creation. It is regarded as incompatible with other human sentiments such as self-surrender, humility, neediness and vulnerability.[2]

On the other hand, the same posture in the context of inter-human relationships can have the opposite meaning: At formal meals or banquets in the ancient Greco-Roman world, for instance, standing was the posture associated with service and hence signaled the status of servantship, subservience, or even slavery. The diners and guests at table reclined or, in some rarer instances, sat. Differences of role and social status were clearly recognized by differences of posture.

STANDING FOR PRAYER IN THE BIBLE. In the context of prayer, standing was the ordinary posture among most ancient peoples—standing with uplifted hands and with eyes fixed in the direction of the rising sun.[3]

In the Hebrew Scriptures, standing is considered the appropriate and customary posture of God in the presence of the believer (see Genesis 18:22) and of the believer in the presence of God (see 1 Samuel 1:26). The posture common to both God and humans in the situation of prayer suggests, of course, that the God of Israel is a conversation-partner. The God of Israel is one with whom one can communicate, engage in dialogue and even "bargain" (see Genesis 18:22–32).[4] Human beings are not required to "efface" themselves, to diminish their being, to disguise their creaturely reality or to deny their vulnerability and need when approaching God in prayer. They may approach God as they would approach other human beings: standing, face-to-face, without embarrassment, explanation or shame (even though they be conscious of smallness, weakness, vulnerability or sin).[5]

22

So ingrained was this sense of standing as the customary and appropriate posture of the believer before God in prayer that the daily Jewish prayer known as the *Tefillah* or the *Shemoneh Esrai* (the "eighteen benedictions") was also called the *Amidah* ("standing"). The *Mishnah* (compiled c. 200 CE but reflecting much earlier practice) makes it clear that standing is the customary and prescribed posture for daily prayer.[6]

In the gospels, standing for prayer is simply assumed unless another posture is noted: "When you stand to pray" (Mark 11:25); "Do not behave like the hypocrites who love to stand and pray in the synagogues" (Matthew 6:5); "The Pharisee stood there and said this prayer. . . . The tax collector stood at some distance, not daring even to raise his eyes to heaven" (Luke 18:11,13). In this last instance, standing is considered appropriate even for a prayer of repentance.

STANDING FOR PRAYER IN THE CHURCH. Aside from the earliest period—when the eucharist in many places was still undistinguishable from the community meal—standing was always the principal posture for both communal and private prayer. Just as the priest at the altar stands before God in reverential readiness, so also do the faith-ful; they are the *circumstantes*.[7]

That this was the familiar posture of Christians of the first centuries is attested to by Clement of Alexandria (†215) and by Origen (†254), who sees in the *orante* the perfect corporeal expression of prayer:

> Even more than stretching out the hands to heaven, one must lift up the soul heavenward. More than raising up the eyes, one must lift up the spirit to God. For there can be no doubt that among a thousand possible positions of the body, outstretched hands and uplifted eyes are to be preferred above all others, so imaging forth in the body those directions of the soul which are fitting in prayer. We are of the opinion that this posture should be preferred, where there is nothing to prevent it, for there are certain circumstances, such as sickness, where we may pray even sitting or lying.[8]

In a remarkable passage from his *Apology*, Tertullian (†220) describes the prayer posture of Christians as itself the best preparation for martyrdom.[9] In praising the dedication of monastics (the "new martyrs") who rise during the night or early in the morning for prayer, Chrysostom (†407) notes this same posture—standing with hands raised.[10] Augustine

(†430) saw in this posture a reminder of the Lord's outstretched hands on the cross and an exhortation to
Christians to stretch out their hands in the works of charity.

> "And in your name I will lift up my hands." Therefore, lift
> up your hands in prayer. Our Lord lifted up his hands on the
> cross for us and extended his hands for us. His hands were
> opened on the cross so that our hands might be opened in
> good works, since his cross won mercy for us. Behold, he
> has lifted up his hands and offered himself as sacrifice for us
> to God, and by that sacrifice has taken away all our sins. Let
> us therefore lift upĬ our hands to God in prayer; lifting our
> hands to God will not be confounded if they are also exer-
> cised in doing good works. For what does one who lifts
> the hands do? Whence is the precept that we should pray
> with hands raised to God? The Apostle says: "Lift up clean
> hands, without wrath and deception." So, when you lift
> your hands to God, they should remind you of your works.[11]

But already by the time of Tertullian, standing for prayer
had acquired the specifically Christian significance of being
a sign of the resurrection and had become firmly linked
with Sundays and Eastertide, the weekly and yearly feasts
of the resurrection:

> In the matter of kneeling, as well, prayer is subject to a
> diversity of observances because of those few who abstain
> from kneeling on Saturdays. Since this dissent is actually a
> cause for concern among the churches, the Lord will give
> the grace so that they will either cease from this practice or
> continue to do so without causing scandal to others. We,
> however, according to the tradition we have received, abstain
> from kneeling only on the day of the Lord's resurrection,
> indeed from every posture and practice of anxiousness,
> postponing all business transactions as well, lest we give
> any place to the devil. The same applies to the time of
> Pentecost, which is distinguished by this same solemnity
> of exultation.[12]

Obviously, then, Christians did kneel but considered this
posture inappropriate for prayer (common or private) on
Sundays and during the 50 days of Easter.[13] As another third-
century writer would explain:

> It is good for us to remember both that we have fallen in sin
> and that we have risen by the grace of Christ. We therefore
> kneel on six days for prayer, as a sign of our fallen state. But
> on the Lord's day, we do not kneel, as a sign of the resurrec-
> tion through which by the grace of Christ we have been
> freed from sin and from death. This custom has its origin in
> apostolic times as the blessed Irenaeus, bishop and martyr of
> Lyons says in the book *De Paschate*, in which he reminds

us that we are not to kneel during Pentecost since it is of the same importance as the Lord's Day.

By the fourth century, the connection between standing and Sundays/Eastertide became a matter of ecclesiastical discipline. Several synods and ecumenical councils, most importantly Nicea I (325), included this rule against kneeling in canonical legislation:

> Since there are some persons who kneel on the Lord's Day and in the days of Pentecost; in order that all things may be observed in like manner in every church, the holy synod has decreed that all should at those times offer up their prayers to God standing.[15]

From the fourth to the eighth centuries there is no lack of witnesses to this rule of standing for prayer.[16] In his *Letter to Januarius*, Augustine makes it clear that standing is an image or *signum* of the resurrection: "The 50 days that are celebrated after the resurrection of the Lord are already the image not of labor but of peace and joy; because during this time the fast is relaxed and we pray standing, which is the image of the resurrection."[17]

In the words of the Venerable Bede (†735), this standing is a foretaste of our own resurrection:

> Rightly do we venerate in the image of a 50-day period the state of our future blessedness, namely by relaxing the fast, by singing Alleluia, by standing for prayer; the most appropriate forebodings of eternal refreshment, praise and resurrection.

He goes on to say that even following Pentecost Sunday, they still do not return to the kneeling position, in honor of the great feast:

> [I]ndeed it is because of this that we do not immediately bend our knees for prayer as soon as the 50 days are completed but also during the following week we implore the Lord while standing.[18]

Through the commentaries of Amalarius of Metz (820–835), the thoughts of Augustine and Bede found their way into nearly all medieval liturgical commentaries from Rabanus Maurus (†842) to William Durandus (†1296).[19]

A remnant of this ancient tradition survives in the Missal of Paul VI. The rubric for the Litany of the Saints at the Easter Vigil states explicitly: "All present stand, *as is customary during the Easter Season.*[20]

SUMMARY. From its origin as the distinguishing characteristic of *homo erectus,* standing erect on two legs has been the posture for the "enactment" of self-confidence, sovereignty and slavery; control, confrontation and confession; parity, partnership, praise and petitionary prayer; respect, revolt, responsibility and resurrection. In and of itself, standing means nothing more or nothing less than standing. But in the context of an entire pattern of social/ritual behavior, it is the enactment of different, even contradictory, attitudes. Although usually considered an inadequate enactment of supplication, it is still the posture of choice for the most intensive intercessory prayer during the Easter season.

PROSTRATION / KNEELING

IN THE GRECO-ROMAN WORLD. The history of those gestures we refer to by such English words as "prostration" and "kneeling" is complex. The earlier Greek and Latin words *(proskynein, adorare)* that underlie the English notion of "worship/adoration/prostration" evolved in such a way that some primitive references were eventually lost (e.g., the primary reference to *kynein,* "kiss" in the compound verb *pros/kynein),* while newer meanings gained prominence (i.e., prostration as a feature of Persian court ceremonial).

Adoration as an act of kissing. The origins of the familiar religious/cultic gestures of adoration—kneeling and prostration—are undoubtedly linked to the ritual *kiss.* The scholarly debate concerning the precise nature of this linkage has centered on the Greek word *proskynein.* The word—which was used in classical, scriptural and liturgical texts—is often translated to such English words as *adore, worship, venerate, revere,* etc. In liturgical rubrics, *proskynein* means *bow,* or *make an act of reverence.*[21] What can be learned from the evolution of this word?

Adoration as action. In classical antiquity, adoration was not primarily an attitude—that is, a mental or psychological reality—but an *action.* This action was "compound," consisting of a kiss, a gesture with the hand and the bowing of the head or the entire body.[22] It was customary among both Greeks and Romans to "venerate" a person (human or divine) by raising the right hand to the lips, kissing it and

26

then "throwing" the kiss *(oscula jacere)* toward the person or image.[23] In his polemical treatise *Contra Rufinam*, St. Jerome (†420) cites a passage from Job that indicates he is still familiar with this ancient enactment of adoration:

> [T]hose who adore have the custom of kissing the hand and bending the head, which the blessed Job refused to do towards the natural elements (which the pagans considered deities) when he declares, "Had I looked upon the sun as it shone, or the moon in the splendor of its progress, and had my heart been secretly enticed to waft them a kiss with my hand; this too would be a crime for condemnation, for I should have denied God Most High." (Job 31:26–28)[24]

Kneeling or kissing the feet?   Berthe M. Marti has demonstrated that when *proskynein* was used in ancient Greek texts to express "worship of the gods," the gesture implied was kissing, not kneeling. Her conclusions shed important light on the history of the ritual gesture:

- A study of the etymology of *proskynein* would seem to prove that its original meaning was "to worship," "to greet respectfully," "*to greet with a kiss.*"[25]

- A great number of passages in classical and later Greek literature show the use of *proskynein* in contexts where *kissing* (the hand, usually) is clearly the gesture implied or actually stated.[26]

- To worship the earth goddess, a different gesture was required. The ancient Greeks did not "throw a kiss" toward the earth, but *bent down and kissed the earth itself.*[27]

- The Greeks often used *prospiptein* ("fall down to or before"), in association with *proskynein,* to indicate a complex gesture of *both* kneeling or prostration and kissing.[28]

- The hand-kissing gesture was certainly part of the religious ritual repertoire of the Romans. Originally, however, there was no relation between the term *adorare* [29] and this gesture of worship. "To describe a kiss waved with the hand in adoration of a god, the Romans used phrases such as *basia iactare, iacere, oscula jacere,* or *manu venerare.* To translate *proskynein* they often used a whole phrase, like Livy's *summisisse se et osculo limen contigisse* [. . . bent over and touched the threshold with a kiss]."[30]

- Eventually, *adorare* did come to be the word regularly used to translate *proskynein,* for obeisance as well as for worship and "greeting with a kiss."[31]

■ To describe obeisance before earthly rulers, both the Greeks and the Romans chose words that were also used for worship of the gods (Greek: *proskynein;* Latin: *adorare*). *Proskynein* was probably chosen by the Greeks to express "adoration" because 1) the gesture of prostration used by Persians before their rulers reminded the Greeks of their own custom of adoring *Gē* (the earth goddess) with prostration and a kiss, and 2) they assumed the Persians regarded their rulers as gods, and the Greeks and Romans attributed to the ceremony of obeisance a similar spirit of reverence.[32] As Marti writes:

> *Proskynein* therefore expressed both the gesture and the feeling which they attributed to their Oriental neighbors. *Adorare* was used regularly for the same ceremony at a rather late period. It is possible that this happened only after the verb had, perhaps through mistaken etymology, come to be associated with a hand-kissing gesture. It then seemed to be the exact translation of the Greek word *proskynein.*[33]

Adoration as an act of prostration or kneeling.

With the passage of time, "adoration" took on new meanings (meanings linked closely to other gestures and postures, such as kneeling and prostration). An example of this posture in Christian iconography is found in the ninth-century mosaic in the narthex of Hagia Sophia, which shows Emperor Leo VI in the posture of "*proskynesis,*" i.e., kneeling, with body inclined and hands stretched toward the feet of Christ enthroned. The transition from "adoration = kiss/hand gesture" to "adoration = kneeling, prostration, posture of 'self-abasement'" is understandable as a result of two developments: 1) Taking to one's knees was the first part of the complex of actions originally designated by *proskynein,* falling to one's knees and bowing or prostrating completely to worship/reverence/adore the earth goddess; and 2) Forms and rituals originally "proper" to the ritual of supplication alone were extended *to the whole cultus.*

Originally, supplication *(hiketeia)* itself had no special social or religious character; only with the passage of time did supplication acquire a religious/social/ritual significance.

> In supplication of the social sort, a criminal pursued by a family or a city, a citizen chased from his homeland or a person vanquished and persecuted sought aid and protection from a powerful personage (a person who might, otherwise, be an *enemy*). Sometimes the fugitive presented himself

directly to that person—as near as possible, usually, to the foyer of that person's house. At other times, the fugitive sought refuge close to a cultic object such as a statue, an altar, a temple or some other sacred enclosure. Usually, the fugitive carried a green branch of olive or laurel, to which bands of wool had been attached—and, having registered his petition by means of it, he dropped it on the ground (as a sign of submission) at the feet of the person with whom he was seeking sanctuary. If he were seeking sanctuary near a sacred monument, the fugitive seized hold of it or sank down before it. He grasped the knees or the chin of the person whose help he was seeking—and he kissed the hands, the knees, the feet. Through these actions, the fugitive became 'inviolable' [asulos], protected . . . by the rite itself, which seemed to have a kind of magical power. A bit later in history, when organized religions began to replace random magic and to reinforce social institutions, the fugitive/suppliant became 'sacred' [hieros] by means of contact with the cultic object. He was thereby protected by the 'gods of supplication' [theoi hikesioi], especially by Zeus, Themis, Apollo or Artemis.[34]

Conclusions. The vocabulary of the ancient world was rather fluid when it came to describing ritual postures or gestures. Thus, for instance, Plato refers to "*euchai . . . hiketeiai . . . prokuliseis . . . proskynēseis*"[35] ("prayers . . . supplications . . . prostrations . . . adorations"). But it is difficult to press these words too much for exact and precise links to *specific* ritual gestures or actions.

Often, the same set of gestures (kissing, prostration, kneeling) is used to manifest attitudes or actions originally attached to *different* occasions. Thus, for instance, sinking to one's knees might imply a gesture of "supplication" or, in other contexts, a gesture of "adoration."

SCRIPTURAL AND EARLY CHRISTIAN EXAMPLES OF THE USE OF PROSKYNEIN AND ITS SYNONYMS IN VARIOUS RITUAL CONTEXTS. By the time the Hebrew Scriptures were translated into Greek, *proskynein* was used in a variety of ritual contexts.

■ Prayer or Worship

Psalm 29:2   *Worship [proskynēsate] the Lord in his holy court.*

Psalm 95: 6   Come, let us *fall down in worship, and prostrate in supplication [proskynēsōmen*

> *kai prospesōmen*] to him, and weep
> before the Lord who made us.

Daniel 6:11–12   Daniel . . . continued his custom of
going home to *kneel in prayer
and give thanks* [*epi ta gonata autou,
kai proseuchomenos kai exomolo-
goumenos*] to God in the upper
chamber three times a day with the
windows open towards Jerusalem."

It seems that "taking to one's knees" is used even more
often for this same general purpose and that it continued to
be used this way in the New Testament (see Acts 9:40;
20:36; 21:5).

■ Adoration/reverence/veneration

Proskynein is used quite often to signify total prostration
as an expression of the most profound worship:

Numbers 22:31   [Balaam] saw the angel of the LORD
standing on the road, a drawn sword
in his hand; *and he bowed down and
fell prostrate on his face* [*kai kypsas
prosekynēsen tō prosōpōn autou*].

II Chronicles 20:18   Jehosaphat *fell on his face,* and
all Judah with those who lived
in Jerusalem *fell down before
the Lord to worship the Lord*
[*Kaikumpsas Iosaphat epi pro-
sopon autou . . . epesan enanti
Kuriou proskynesai Kuriou*].
(See also II Chronicles 29:29–30;
Esther 3:2,5; Acts 10:25.)

But the first part of the act of prostration, namely "bending"
or "falling on the knees," is used just as often to express
veneration/reverence/adoration for God or for persons:

Isaiah 45:23   To me, *every knee shall bend* [*kampsei
pan gonu*].

Matthew 27:29   *And bending their knees* [*kai gony-
petēsantes*] before him they mocked
him saying: Hail, King of the Jews.
(See also Mark 10:17; Luke 5:8;

Romans 11:4; Philippians 2:10;
Ephesians 3:14.)

■ Supplication, petition, intensive prayer

The scriptures never use *proskynein* in the context of supplication. This is understandable in light of the origin of
the rite of supplication described above. What we see
emphasized instead is the action of taking to or falling to
one's knees:

> 1 Kings 8:54 When Solomon finished offering this
> entire prayer of petition to the LORD he
> rose from before the altar *where he
> had been kneeling [epi ta gonata]* with
> his hands outstretched toward heaven.
> (See also II Kings 1:13; Ezra 9:5)

> Mark 1:40 A leper came to him *and pleaded on his
> knees [kai gonypetōn]*: "If you want to,"
> he said, "you can cure me." (See Matthew
> 17:14; Luke 22:41)

These examples show that a word like *proskynein*—even
when used in ritual contexts and even when presumed to
have a single cultic significance—may still carry a variety
of meanings as to posture, gesture, action and (internal)
attitude. The same holds true for the various references to
kneeling, properly speaking *(tithemi ta gonata, klempsei ta
gonata, gonypetein),* which had become an important ritual
gesture often used as a synonym or in conjunction with
proskynein. Both kneeling and prostration could enact the
attitudes of worship/veneration/adoration and prayer, but
the primary or exclusive meaning of kneeling seems to have
been supplication and petition.

KNEELING FOR PRAYER IN THE LITURGY. In spite
of the diversity of meanings associated with prostration
and kneeling in the scriptures, the two postures were soon
distinguished from one another in liturgical practice and
understood to enact different attitudes in prayer. Prostration,
most obviously in the East, became more and more associated with adoration, while kneeling—true to its origin and
exclusive meaning in the scriptures—became primarily
associated with intensive supplication, penitence and non-
festive prayer rather than with prayer in general. This

was undoubtedly the reason behind the legislation prohibiting kneeling on Sundays and during Pentecost. But kneeling was considered proper and fitting—if not required—on certain occasions, just as it was forbidden on Sundays. Tertullian, in the passage already quoted with regard to standing, makes the case for kneeling and sets down the tradition he wishes to hand on:

> But on ordinary days, who would hesitate to fall prostrate before God, at least during that first prayer with which we enter upon the light of day? However, on fast days and stational days, no prayer is to be made without kneeling and the rest of the customary marks of humility: for on those days to God, our Lord.[36]

However, there was not always a clear distinction between complete prostration and kneeling: The council of Neo-Caesarea (314) speaks of the penitents as those who kneel *(gonu klinon),*[37] while canon 11 of Nicea (325) calls them the *prostrati (hypopesountai).*[38]

The early liturgical books of the West, especially the sacramentaries (prayer texts), *ordines* (ceremonial directives or rubrics), and pontificals (bishop's books), provide extensive evidence of the penitential/supplicatory nature of kneeling.

Sacramentaries. Although it contains no rubrics whatsoever, the oldest collection of prayer texts of the Roman church, the *Veronense,*[39] uses the image of kneeling or prostrating during some of the presidential prayers to convey precisely the attitude of humility or penitence.[40] These prayer texts suppose that kneeling for prayer is familiar, but it is improbable that one would have actually knelt while saying (or hearing) these presidential prayers in the context of public worship.

The so-called Gelasian Sacramentary[41] contains a few rubrics, the first of which appears under the title *Ordo agentibus publicam paenitentiam* (n. 83), and calls not for simple kneeling but for full prostration: "And when [the penitent] has prostrated his entire body on the ground, the pontiff says the prayer for reconciliation over him."[42]

In the rubrics for Good Friday, the Gelasian provides some of the oldest evidence of communal kneeling for intensive, supplicatory prayer that would virtually characterize Lent, Embertides and other penitential days until the Missal of Paul VI: "The priest says: 'Let us pray'; then the deacon

32

announces, 'Let us kneel'; and after a short pause he says, 'Let us stand.' And the priest says the oration."[43] The same diaconal directives are given after each of the biddings of the solemn intercessions (nos. 400–416), a practice that survives on Good Friday in the Missal of Paul VI.[44]

The famous "Gregorian" sacramentary sent by Pope Hadrian to Charlemagne in 785 contained, apart from its brief *ordo missae* at the beginning, no rubrics at all. Those who wished to use the book had to make use of the *ordines romani.* One prayer, a *super populum* for Ash Wednesday, refers to bowing before the majesty of God, not unrelated to the attitude we have seen attached to kneeling or prostration:

> Look graciously, Lord,
> *upon those who bow before your majesty,*
> so that those who have been restored by the divine gift
> may always be nourished by heavenly assistance.[45]

When the prayer was composed, the *super populum* was undoubtedly prayed over bowed heads *(inclinantes).* At the time the text was transcribed at Charlemagne's court, the people may have been kneeling as well as bowing their heads for this prayer.

Ordines Romani *and Pontificals.* The *ordines* (collections of ceremonial directives) are among the earliest witnesses to the gestures, postures and movements of the Roman Rite. Although the compilation of many was complete only in the eighth century, some *ordines* describe celebrations at the time of Gregory I (590–604) or earlier. One of the oldest, in use about the same time as the Gelasian Sacramentary, notes that the pope "prostrates himself before the altar for prayer" at the beginning of the synaxis on Good Friday.[46]

The same *ordo* also describes the *"Flectamus genua"* of the solemn intercessions that we have already seen.[47] When this same rubric is described in the 10th-century pontifical, an added phrase, "and he prays a short while," indicates that this prayer on the knees was not the perfunctory genuflection it would become in modern times; at that time it still retained its significance as a time for silent prayer—intensified supplication—on the part of the entire assembly.[48]

Ordo XXII, compiled in Francia in the last decade of the eighth century,[49] indicates that kneeling was a matter of course on the weekdays of Lent. The deacon's invitation appears before the oration at the *collecta* and again before the opening prayer at the station where Mass is to be celebrated.[50] The deacon also commands the assembly: "*Humiliate capita vestra* [Bow your heads]," before the *oratio super populum* ("prayer over the people") at the end of the Lenten Masses. The ordo also specifies:

> The same manner [of praying] is done on Mondays, Wednesdays, Fridays and Saturdays throughout Lent. [We do this] on Saturdays only since the time Pope Hadrian established that kneelings be done for King Charles. Indeed before [Hadrian's order], this was not the custom.[51]

Apparently Pope Hadrian made quite a point of extending the practice of kneeling for intercessory prayer, especially on behalf of Charlemagne, the *Patricius Romanorum* (Noble Patron of the Romans): In one of his letters, the pope mentions some who "implore our God on bended knees shouting 300 Kyries in loud voices without ceasing" on Charlemagne's behalf.[52]

Given the use of kneeling on penitential days, it is not surprising that kneeling has a prominent place in the rite for the reconciliation of penitents. The Romano-Germanic Pontifical specifies that on Ash Wednesday, "after the deacon has said '*Flectamus genua*,' the [*oratio*] *super populum* is prayed with their heads bowed. . . . [T]hen the priest should admonish all . . . that they proceed hastily to genuine confession and to true penitence."[53] Among the penitential practices, the rite includes "frequent kneeling,"[54] and later,

> [a]fter the confession and admonition, he [the penitent] bends his knees to the earth and then standing again, reaches out in supplication with an expression of regret and lament, and looking to the priest, he says these words . . . Once the confession is finished, he prostrates himself on the ground and produces from the inmost heart weeping, sighs, and tears, as much as God shall give. The priest shall wait for him for a little while to remain prostrate as he can see him moved to compunction by divine inspiration. Then the priest orders him to rise and, when he has stood upon his feet, he shall wait with trembling and humility for the judgment (penance) of the priest.[55]

This manner of kneeling, standing, prostrating and standing as an expression of humility and readiness to do penance is repeated again in solemn fashion at the service of the reconciliation of penitents on Holy Thursday (nos. 228–251).

34

KNEELING AS VENERATION AND ADORATION. In the first millennium, kneeling for communal prayer was limited to days without festive character. The liturgical and extra-liturgical sources quoted thus far indicate that the posture is most closely associated with penitence and intensive supplication or intercession. Its later association with veneration and adoration undoubtedly evolved as prostration/kissing became less and less common as expressions of veneration (in the West) and as kneeling began to replace full prostration in a number of ritual contexts.

Veneration of the cross. The clearest evidence of this evolution is perhaps the successive descriptions of the veneration of the cross on Good Friday. *Ordo XXIII,* the earliest description of the ceremony at Rome, indicates that the veneration was preceded by a procession with the relic of the cross from the Lateran to Santa Croce.

> And when they reach Jerusalem [i.e, Santa Croce], they enter the church and the deacon places the *capsa* containing the cross on the altar, and then the pope opens it. Then he prostrates himself before the altar to pray, and afterwards rises, kisses the cross and goes to stand near the chair. And at his signal, the bishops, presbyters, deacons and subdeacons kiss the cross upon the altar. Then they place it on the small box at the chancel gates where the rest of the people kiss it.[56]

Note that the prostration for prayer and the veneration with a kiss are separate actions; the others who venerate do not prostrate first. Furthermore, there is an obvious parallel between the prostration for prayer at the beginning of the Good Friday synaxis and the standing/inclining for prayer at the beginning of the papal Mass described in *Ordo I.* The prostration/praying belongs to the entrance rite; the kissing is the act of veneration of the cross. Both gestures enact adoration, honor and respect.

While in *Ordo XXIII* the rite of veneration was followed by the readings and solemn prayers (with kneeling for silent prayer after each bidding as described above), its presbyteral adaptation (Gelasian Sacramentary), and the early Frankish adaptations *(Ordines XXIV, XXVII, and XXVIII)*, place the veneration after the intercessions:

> Following the prayers, the cross is prepared a small distance in front of the altar, suspended on either side by two acolytes. After an *oratorium* is placed in front of it, the *pontifex*

comes and adores and so kisses the cross [(or) adores the cross with a kiss]. Next the bishops, presbyters, deacons and the rest in their respective order, then the people.[57]

The placing of the *oratorium* (mentioned also at the beginning of Mass in *Ordo I*) implies that the pontiff still prostrates or at least prays before kissing the cross. The silent prayer (with prostration on the most solemn occasions), which was a normal part of the entrance rite, was transferred along with the preparation of the cross to the rite of veneration when it was moved to its new place after the prayers. The text is silent about what happens *on the oratorium* (prostration? kneeling? adoration? prayer?), but it definitely indicates that *the kiss* is the act of adoration: *et adoratam deosculatur crucem.*

Ordo XXX-A, on the other hand, emphasizes the prostration or kneeling as the act of venerating the cross; the kiss is added to it and followed by communion from the reserved sacrament: "At the end of the orations, all adore the holy cross, kiss it and communicate from the *Sancta* that remains from the previous day."[58] *Ordo XXX-B* abbreviates this further: "And all adore the holy cross and are communicated."[59]

In the mid-tenth century, when the Romano-Germanic Pontifical was compiled, the Roman prostration was replaced by a three-fold genuflection (as indicated by three devotional prayers, entitled *Oratio ad crucem domini in prima genuflexione . . . in secunda genuflexione, in tertia genuflexione*).[60] This pontifical, transplanted to Rome during the Ottonian reform (960s–1002), was highly influential in many regards, but its three genuflections could not supplant the older custom of prostration. The two ideas were combined and expanded in the Roman pontificals compiled during the twelfth century:

> After the oration, according to the custom of the Roman church, a tapestry is spread in front of the altar; a cross covered with linen is placed on it at the foot of the altar. Then, the barefoot pontiff approaches first by himself to adore it while the ministers stand on either side holding it. He is to make a complete prostration three times on the tapestry so that after the third prostration he is right at the cross and can then humbly and devoutly kiss it.

> Then he takes the cross and rises [sic] and reverently sings three times the entire antiphon *Ecce lignum crucis* [*Behold the wood of the cross*] . . . In this antiphon where it says

> *Venite adoremus* [*Come, let us adore*], he and all the clergy and people are to humbly kneel.
>
> The cantors, according to their custom, sing *Agios* etc., *Sanctus Deus*, etc. [Holy God, Holy Mighty One. . . .]. Whenever *miserere nobis* [*have mercy on us*] is said, all are to prostrate on the earth.[61]

The Roman Pontificals of the thirteenth century abbreviated the rubric, assuming everyone knew the basic form of the rite: "And then all prostrate on the tapestry and pray for a while."[62]

With the Pontifical of William Durandus (†1296), the Good Friday service reached the definitive form it would have until the reform of Holy Week in the 1950s:[63] the prostration of the clergy at the entrance, readings and intercessions, and then veneration of the cross beginning with the three-fold showing and three-fold genuflection that first appeared in the tenth century.

Summary.   In the earliest description of the veneration of the cross, the act of prostration and the act of kissing were separate expressions of veneration. The former was done only by the pope, and the latter—considered the actual "venerating" of the cross—was done by all. Gradually, the two gestures were fused, at least in the rubrical descriptions, so that the prostration and kissing were together considered the act of veneration. It was the Franco-Germanic replacement of prostration with "prayers on the knees" that put kneeling in the context of "veneration"—a place where we had not previously seen it in the liturgical documents. While kneeling did not immediately supplant prostration as the preferred act of veneration to be joined to the kiss, it did become an alternate expression of adoration assumed by the entire assembly in response to the *Venite adoremus* of the antiphon *Ecce lignum.* Eventually, if not already by the twelfth century, everyone would always kneel at *Venite adoremus*—as during the singing of the invitatory Psalm 94/95 at the beginning of each day's office.

HONOR OF PERSONS.   Of course, the simultaneous evolution of the signs of honor and respect before the pope and other bishops also played a role in the association of kneeling with adoration. Borrowed from the imperial court, the custom of kissing the feet of the pope made its appearance by the end of the seventh century. *Ordo Romanus I* directs the deacon who is to read the gospel to first "kiss the feet of the pope, then go before the altar and kiss the Book of the Gospels."[64] The ancient kiss is the primary expression of reverence in both cases, but the fact that one had to get down on one's knees in order to reach the foot of the pope meant that this part of the gesture came to share in the enactment of respect. Later descriptions of pontifical and episcopal liturgies will show the omission of the kiss but the survival of the genuflection.[65]

KNEELING: WORSHIP OF THE EUCHARIST. By the time the new cult of the eucharist had fully blossomed in the thirteenth century, the ancient liturgical enactment of penitence and intensive supplication had acquired from prostration additional overtones of veneration, respect and honor. It was a short step from veneration of the cross to adoration of Christ present in the eucharist. But, as we shall see in Chapter Four, it would be a long time before kneeling, or its abbreviated form in the single genuflection, would be primarily linked to adoration of the reserved sacrament and considered a fitting posture for the eucharistic prayer.

But before continuing our discussion of the evolution of posture during the eucharistic prayer itself, it would be helpful to examine the social and theological significance of posture and gesture in the eucharistic practice of the early church. This entails an examination of the meal ministry of Jesus as well, for it is only in light of the gospel that we can understand what "inner spirit" should be "expressed and fostered" by the postures we assume during the great thanksgiving.

ENDNOTES

1. The formal restaurant is the clearest example of the distinction between those who feast and those who serve; at large family gatherings, the adults are often separated from the children when all cannot sit around one table; fast food establishments try to blur (or at least shield us) from these distinctions by having the customer carry his/her own food to a location separate from the "serving area"—yet the "buspersons" still *stand* to render the services of cleaning tables and floors or removing trays left by "negligent" customers.

2. Recall the gospel story of the Pharisee and the publican. The Pharisee's posture represents the significance of standing at its arrogant worst; on the other hand, the publican is also standing but without arrogant self-righteousness.

3. Frederich Heiler, *Das Gebet: Eine religionsgeschichtliche und religionspsychologische Untersuchungen*, 4th ed. (Munich, 1923); S. McComb, trans. and ed., *Prayer: A Study in the History and Psychology of Religion* (New York: Oxford University Press, 1958).

4. A similar relationship is expressed by the Hebrew Bible's frequent references to the physical gesture/posture of "turning one's eyes to God." This gesture/posture (see, for example, 2 Chronicles 20:12; Psalm 25:15) suggests that, in biblical revelation, one encounters God in prayer through a face-to-face meeting.

5. See Psalm 34:5–6: "Look towards God and be radiant; let your faces not be abashed. This poor man called, and the Lord heard him and rescued him from all his distress." Numerous psalms speak of "seeking the face of God" e.g., 24:6; 42:3; 80:4, 8, 20. On standing for prayer in the Hebrew Scriptures, see also Exodus 33:8; 1 Samuel 1:26; Psalm 134:2; regarding "listening" to God see Exodus 19:17; Nehemiah 8:5.

6. See *Mishnah Berakoth*, 1.3; 3.5; 4.5; 5.1; in Herbert Danby, ed., *The Mishnah* (Oxford, 1933), 2–5.

7. Josef A. Jungmann, *The Mass of the Roman Rite* [MRR], 2 vols. (New York: Benziger, 1955; reprint Westminister, 1986), I: 239–240; see also II: 166. Jungmann notes that in Switzerland, even after 1500, it was customary for the faithful to pray with arms outstretched from the consecration until communion. On standing with arms raised in prayer, cf. Quasten, *Monumenta* 174, n. 4, on his commentary on Ambrose, *De sacramentis* VI. 4, 17. In the early church, all the postures and gestures of prayer that were done in common were done likewise in private; on this see Robert Taft, *The Liturgy of the Hours in East and West* (Collegeville: The Liturgical Press, 1986), 29.

8. Origen, *De Oratione*, 31, 2; P. Koetschau, *Die Griechischen Christlichen Schriftsteller der ersten drei Jahrhunderte* (Berlin: Akademie Verlag, 1899), III: 267. Another English translation can be found in R.A. Greer, *Origen*, Classics of Western Spirituality (New York: Paulist, 1979), 164–65.

9. *Apology*, XXX; PL 1:503–504; CCL 1:141–142: "To [heaven we] Christians lift our eyes—with hands outstretched, because they are harmless; with head uncovered, because we are not ashamed; and indeed without a prayer-monitor, because we pray from the heart. We pray ceaselessly for all the emperors, that they may have long life; for the empire, that it may know security. . . . With hands thus stretched out to God, let their hooves trample us, let their crosses suspend us, their flames lick us, their swords remove our heads, their wild beasts pounce on us; the very pasture of a Christian at prayer is preparation for every form of torture." Another English translation in E.J. Davy, *Tertullian: Apologetical Works*, Fathers of the Church, X: 85–86.

10. See *Hom. XIV in Tim 1:5*; PG 62: 575. Standing for prayer with outstretched hands is attested to well into the Middle Ages, especially among monastic writers: Ambrose, *De Virginibus*, I:2 in PL 16: col. 201 and II:4 in PL 16: col. 225; Adamnan, *Vita Columbae* l. II, c. 31; *Rule of Maelruain*, in W. Reeves, *The Culdees of the British Islands* (Dublin, 1864), 87; Gregory of Tours, *Vitae Patrum* c. 20; PL 71: col. 1093; *Constitutiones Camaldoli*, 1253, edit. Mittarelli et Costadone, Venice 1755–73, t. VI, 2e pt. col. 3. Gregory describes Benedict standing with arms outstretched as he breathed his last; see *Dialogi de vita*, 2:37; for an English translation see O. Zimmerman and B. Avery, *Life and Miracles of St. Benedict* (Collegeville: The Liturgical Press, 1980), 75.

11. Sancti Aurelii Augustini, *Ennarationes in Psalmos*, Ennaratio in Psalmum LXII, 13; CCL 39: 801–802.

12. Q. Septimi Florentis Tertulliani, *De Oratione liber*, c. 23; see Ernest Evans, ed., *Tertullian's Tract on Prayer* (London: SPCK, 1953), 32. See also *De Corona militis* 3, 4; PL II:79–80: "*Die dominico ieiunare nefas ducimus vel de geniculis adorare. Eadem immunitate a die Paschae in Pentecosten usque gaudemus.* [We count fasting or kneeling on the Lord's day to be unlawful. We rejoice in the same privilege as well from Easter to Pentecost]."

13. Peter of Alexandria († 311) prohibits kneeling on Sundays in canon 25 of his synod after 307.

14. Ps-Justin, *Quaestiones ad orthodoxos*, q. 115; PG 6: col. 1363.

15. Charles J. Hefele and Henri Leclercq, *Histoire des Conciles*, 11 vols. (Paris: Letouzey et Ane, 1907–1952), I:I, 528–620; W. Bright, *Canons of the First Four Councils*, 2nd. ed., pp. ix–xv, 1–89, quoted in J. Stevenson, ed., *A New Eusebius* (London: SPCK, 1968), 364.

16. Among others, Hilary of Poitiers († 367), *Prologus in Psalmos*, n. 12; Epiphanius of Salamis (†403), *Expositio fidei*, n. 22; Basil of Caesarea († 379), *De Spiritu Sancto*, c. 61 (sometimes numbered 27); Jerome († ca. 420), *Dialogus contra Luciferianos*, c. 4 and the *Proemium* on the Epistle to the Ephesians; Maximus of Turin († 465), *Homilia III de Pentecostes*; John Cassian

(†435), *Institutiones Cæno-biorum*, Book II, c. 18; *Collationes*, XXI, n. 20; canon 57 of the Council of Braga (563) and canon 90 of the Council in Trullo (691).

17. *Epistula 55 ad Januarium*, 15:28, *Corpus scriptorum ecclesiasticorum* [CSEL] 34/2: 202. Quoted by Amalarius, *Liber Officialis*, I: 36, 2; J.M. Hanssens, ed., *Amalarii episcopi Opera Liturgica Omnia*, 3 vols. (Studi e Testi 138–140), II. See also Augustine *Ep.*55, 17, 32 in CSEL 34/2: 207. Basil makes a similar reference to Sunday in *De Spiritu sancto* 27, referred to in J. Daniélou, *The Bible and the Liturgy*, (Notre Dame, IN: University of Notre Dame Press, 1956), 263f.

18. Venerable Bede, Homily II, 16; CCL 122: 298. Quoted by Amalarius in *Liber Officialis* I, 37; J. M. Hanssens, ed., *Amalarii episcopi Opera Liturgica Omnia*, (Studi e Testi 139), II: 178–179.

19. Rabanus Maurus (†842), *De institutione Clericorum*. II, 42; PL 110: 190D–191A; ed. Alois Knöpfler, p. 143; Pseudo-Hugo of St. Victor (ca. 1140), *Speculum de mysteriis Ecclesiae*; PL 177: 346A; Sicard of Cremona (†1215), *Mitrale seu de officiis ecclesiaticis summa*, VI:15; PL 213: 351BC and later at VII, 11:; PL 213: 385A. Durandus (†1296) quotes Sicard on this in VI, 113, 8; *Rationale divinorum officiorum*, V. 5, 16; VI. 1, 11: *Et quandoque stamus, quasi laetantes, quod in domum Domini ibimus.* We stand for Easter, Pentecost, the feasts of the angels and saints, and during Christmas season: (Easter) *stantes oramus propter laetitiam resurrectionis, quam tunc recolimus;* (on Pentecost) *recolimus libertatem per adventum Spiritus sancti nobis datam;* (on feasts) *recolimus sanctam societatem Angelorum et sanctorum, quae iam est in laetitia sempiterna;* (Christmas time) *tempus regressionis quod est tempus gaudii.* John Beleth (†1182) ordered standing for prayer during the Easter season, the *tempus gaudii . . . et reconciliationis;* see *Rationale divinorum officiorum*, 56; PL 202: 62D and *Rationale*, 121;, PL 202: 128B; Honorius of Autun (†ca. 1152) explained the obligation of standing for prayer on Sundays: "During paschaltide we pray standing since we do not pray during this season for the public penitents, since the church has already opened her doors to them." *Sacramentarium seu de causis et significatu mystico rituum divini in ecclesia officia liber*, 4; PL 172: 742B.

20. *Missal Romanum*, Editio Typica (Typis Polyglottis Vaticanis, 1971), 281, n. 39: *Et canuntur litaniae a duobus cantoribus, omnibus stantibus (propter tempus paschale) et respondentibus.*

21. As in the Divine Liturgy of St. John Chrysostom: "The deacon, making a single reverence [*proskynēsas hapax*], receives the holy cup from the priest."

22. See C. Daremberg and E. Saglio, ed., *Dictionnaire des Antiquities grecques et romaines*, (Paris: Librairie Hachette), I/1:80; *s.v.* "Adoratio, Prokynesis."

23. This gesture is depicted in ancient sculptures, vase paintings and murals; see examples

in Daremberg-Saglio, *Dict. des antiquites*, I/1, pp. 80–81. The same gesture is described in Pliny the Elder (†79 CE), *Historia naturalis*, bk. 28, ch. 5: "*In adorando dextram ad osculum referimus totumque corpus circumagimus* [In adoring we give a kiss to our right hand and twist our whole body around]." See A. Ernout, ed., *Pline l'Ancien. Histoire Naturelle. Livre XXVIII* (Paris: Société d'Edition "Les Belles Lettres," 1962), 26.

24. *Contra Rufinam*, Bk. 1, ch. 19. Latin text may be found in P. Lardet, ed., Saint Jérôme: *Apologie contre Rufin*, Sources Chrétiennes 303 (Paris: Cerf, 1983), 54.

25. Berthe M. Marti, "Proskynesis and Adorare," *Language* 12 (1936): 272–82; here, 273.

26. E.g., as a formulaic apology for indiscreet words (so Plato in the *Republic*); as a formula of "blessing" against the bad omen of sneezing (so Aristotle in the *Problemata*; compare our modern habit of saying "Bless you!" or "Gesundheit!" when someone sneezes); as a gesture of worship toward the heavenly bodies (chiefly the sun and moon; so the passage in the book of Job, cited above). See Marti, 273–277 for texts and discussion.

27. So, for instance, Homer describes Ulysses doing this upon his return to his native land: Odyssey 5.462–463: "... *ho d'ek potamoio liastheis / schoinoi hypeklinthe, kuse de zeidoron arouran.*" The word Homer used was "*kysein* [kiss]," but a later scholiast explained

the term—and the gesture—by the word "*proskynein.*" See discussion in Marti, 277.

28. "Thus the verb *proskynein* was used to describe a gesture of reverence of which a kiss was properly a part." Marti, 279.

29. It should be noted, however, that originally, *adorare* had no connection with *os* and no connection with a hand-kissing gesture. Instead, the verb *adorare* appears to belong to the group of words meaning "to pronounce words of a solemn character . . . The verbal prefix *ad* is often used as an intensive with no idea of motion toward, as . . . in the verbs *adaugeo, acduro, adformido, adiuro.*" Marti, 280. Originally, then, *adorare* (like *orare*) seems to have meant "*causam agere,*" i.e., to pronounce the solemn words of a legal or religious formula. By extension (working from the notion of "pronouncing words of a solemn character"), *adorare* became a synonym of *colere, venerari* ("worship," "venerate / revere"). It is used in this latter sense by authors like Livy: "*deos immortales ita adoravi . . . ut mihi . . . gloriam . . . darent.*" Text in C.F. Walters and R.S. Conway, eds., *Titi Livi Ab Urbe Condita* (Oxford, 1919). See also another passage from Livy's histories, where the activities of King Prusias at Rome (c. 166 BCE) are described: " . . . *cum veniret in curiam, summisisse se et osculo limen curiae contigisse . . .* " Text in P. Jal, ed., *Tite-Live, Histoire Romaine; Livre XLV* (Paris: Société d'Édition "Les Belles Lettres," 1979), 72.

30. Marti, 281.

31. The earliest usage of *adorare* in this evolved sense is the passage from Pliny the Elder quoted earlier in these notes. Marti collects texts and comments on them, pp. 281–282.

32. See A. E. Crawley, "Kissing" in James Hastings, ed., *Encyclopedia of Religions and Ethics* (New York: Scribners, 1955), VII:742. The adoration offered Roman emperors was influenced by oriental (especially Persian) ceremonial. It consisted in bowing or kneeling, touching the robe and putting the hand to the lips, or kissing the robe. A variation was the kissing of the emperor's feet or knees. This custom of adoration does not seem to have become the fashion until the time of Diocletian (emperor from 284 to 305 CE).

33. Marti, 282.

34. A. Delatte, "Le baiser, l'agenouillement et le prosternement de l'adoration (προσκυνησις) chez les Grecs," *Bulletin de la Classe de Lettres et des Sciences Morales et Politiques* (Académie royale de Belgique), 37 (1951): 423–44, here 442. Delatte then provides a variety of historical references to this "rite of supplication" as it had emerged in social/religious contexts. See pp. 442–444.

35. Plato, Laws, Book 10; 887 E: " . . . they carried on a dialogue in prayers and supplications with gods . . . At the rising of the sun and moon, and at their settings, they heard of and saw Greeks and all the barbarians . . . kneeling and prostrating [*proskyneseis te kai orontes*] themselves . . . " T. Pangle, *The Laws of Plato* (New York: Basic Books, 1980), 283–84.

36. Q. Septimi Florentis Tertulliani, *De Oratione liber.* c. 23 Trans: JKL. Latin text and another translation may be found in Ernest Evans, ed., *Tertullian's Tract on Prayer* (London: SPCK, 1953), 32.

37. Canon 5; from Charles Hefele and Henri Leclercq, *Histoire des Conciles, I:I,* 326–334.

38. See Charles Hefele and Henri Leclercq, *Histoire des Conciles, I:I,* 528–620.

39. Verona, Bilioteca Capitolare codex 85, a sixth-century document formerly known as the Leonine sacramentary; cf. C. Vogel, *Medieval Liturgy: An Introduction to the Sources* (Washington: Pastoral Press), 38–46.

40. L. C. Mohlberg, et al., eds., *Sacramentarium Veronense,* Rerum Ecclesiasticarum Documenta, Series Major, Fontes 1 (Rome: Herder, 1956), nos. 136, 446, 448, 916.

41. *Vaticanus Reginensis codex* 316, mid-eighth-century copy of a 7th-century compilation; cf. Vogel, *Medieval Liturgy,* 64–70. The manuscript has been edited by L.C. Mohlberg, et al., *Liber Sacramentorum Romanæ Æcclesiæ ordinis anni circuli,* Rerum Ecclesiasticarum Documenta, Series Major 4 (Rome, 1960).

42. *. . . et prostrato eo omni corpore, in terram, dat orationem pontifex super eum ad reconciliandum.* The rubric is repeated again at n. 352 for the reconciliation of penitents on Holy Thursday.

43. *Et . . . sacerdos . . . dicit*
Oremus. *Et adnuntiat diaconus:*
Flectamus genua. *Et post
paulolum dicit* Levate. *Et dat
orationem* (no. 395).

44. The Solemn Prayer for-
mat—consisting of the bidding
or invitation, the silence in
which the entire assembly
prayed or rather in which the
Spirit prayed through the entire
assembly, and then the concluding prayer voiced by the
bishop or presbyter—is one of
the most ancient forms of
Christian public prayer. During
Lent and on other penitential
days, the penitential and supplicatory character of the silent
prayer was intensified by the
posture of kneeling. See Robert
Taft, *Beyond East and West*
(Washington, DC: Pastoral
Press, 1984), 151–164, adapted
from an article that first
appeared in *Worship* 52 (1978):
314–329.

45. *Inclinantes se domine
maiestati tuae propitiatus
intende, ut qui diuino munere
sunt refecti, caelestibus semper
nutriantur auxiliis. Per
dominum. . . .* See J. Deshusses,
Le Sacramentarie grégorien,
Spicilegium Friburgense 16
(Fribourg, 1971). Hadrianum, n.
157; Paduense, n. 131.

46. *. . . prosternit se ante
altare ad orationem; Ordo
Romanus* [OR] 23: 13; *Les
Ordines Romani du haut
moyen age,* M. Andrieu, ed., 5
vols, Spicilegium Sacrum
Lovaniense 11, 23, 24, 28, 29
(Louvain: 1931–1961), III: 271;
cf, OR 24: 23; OR 27: 36. That
"ad orationem" should be
translated "for prayer" rather
than "for the oration" is clari-
fied in the 10th-century
Romano-Germanic Pontifical

[PRG]: *prostrato omni corpore
in terra diutius* (PRG XCIX:
304); C. Vogel and R. Elze, eds.,
*Le Pontifical Romano-
Germanique du dixième siècle,*
Studie Testi 226–227 (Vatican
City, 1963), II:86.

47. OR XXIII:20; OR XXIV:1–3;.

48. PRG XCIX: 308–311. The
ordines for Embertides (PRG
XCIX) and the Greater Litanies
(OR XXI) also indicate kneeling
for the orations after each of
the readings or for the various
stations in the Rogations. *Per
singulas orationes in XII lec-
tiones genuflectimus, excepto
in octavis pentecostes. In sola
de camino ignis, genua non
flectimus;* PRG XCIX: 448, 449,
450; edit. Vogel-Elze, II:
134–135. Cf. OR XXI: 8, 13;
Michel Andrieu, ed., *Les
Ordines Romani,* III: 247–49.

49. M. Andrieu, ed., *Les
Ordines Romani,* III: 259–262.
See the discussion of this Ordo
in A. Chavasse, *Le Sacramen-
taire gélasien* (Vat. Reg., 316),
(Paris-Tournai, 1958), 87–137,
215–272; a further bibliography
in C. Vogel, *Medieval Liturgy*
(Washington DC: Pastoral
Press, 1986), 217, n. 123.

50. After 731, every day during
Lent was an occassion for a stational celebration of the eucharist. The people and clergy
would gather at one church (the
collecta) and process to the
"stational" church for the readings and rest of Mass. For further information on the
stational liturgies of Lent see,
among others, John F. Baldovin,
*The Urban Character of Chris-
tian Worship in Jerusalem,
Rome, and Constantinople,*
Orientalia Christiana Analecta
228 (Rome, 1987).

51. Nos. 12–13. On the phrase regarding Charlemagne see J. A. Jungmann, *'Flectere pro Carole rege,'* *Mélanges Andrieu* (Strasbourg, 1956), 219–228.

52. *Codex Carolinus* 51: " . . . *Trecentos 'kyrieleyson' extensis vocibus . . . Deo nostro adclamandum non cessant flexis genibus exorantes.*"

53. "*Feria IV in capite ieiunii . . . 'Flectamus genua' pronuntiate diacono super populum cum inclinatione capitis, . . . premonere debet sacerdos omnes . . . , quatinus ad veram confessionem veramque paenitentiam festinantius accedant*"; PRG XCIX: 44.

54. "*. . . sepius flectendo genua*"; PRG XCIX: 47.

55. PRG XCIX: nos. 52, 54.

56. OR XXIII:13–14.

57. OR XXIV:30 = XXVII:42 = XXVIII:39. OR XXIX:35 uses the same phrase.

58. OR XXXA:10.

59. OR XXXB:35.

60. PRG XCIX: 330-333.

61. *Pontificale Romanum* [PR] XIIs, 31:7–9: *Le Pontifical romain au moyen âge,* Michel Andrieu, ed., 4 vols., Studi e Testi 86–88, 99 (Citta del Vaticano: Biblioteca Apostolica Vaticana, 1938), I: 236.

62. PR XIIIs. 43:6; Michel Andrieu, ed., *Le Pontifical romain,* II: 465.

63. Michel Andrieu, ed., *Le Pontifical romain,* III: 582–585.

64. OR I: 59.

65. The kissing of the foot, hand, knees, right shoulder, breast and mouth of the pope or bishop appears along with the genuflection before the prelate as late as the Pontifical of William Durandus (†1296); see the index in Michel Andrieu, ed., *Le Pontifical romain,* IV: 323–324, for a complete listing of references. The *Cæremoniale Episcoporum* (I, 18, 3.), in use until Vatican II, directed that the clergy genuflect whenever they pass before the bishop.

CHAPTER THREE OUTLINE

I. Banquet customs in the ancient world

  A. Postures

  B. Ranking guests at table

  C. Washing

II. The ideology of banquets

  A. Social bonding

  B. Social obligation

  C. Social stratification

  D. Social equality

III. The New Testament banquet

  A. Last Supper tradition

  B. The "meal ministry" of Jesus and the meals of the early Christians

IV. Paul and the meals at Antioch

V. The "Lord's Supper" at Corinth

VI. Conclusions

Ritual Posture in the Context of Meals and the Meal Ministry of Jesus | 3

The fact that Christians ate together when they met as a community is a characteristic they shared with virtually the entire ancient world. For the ancients, the meal was a social institution shared in common throughout the culture, regardless of any social, ethnic or religious distinctiveness a group otherwise might have. All meals in the ancient world have to be seen as *manifestations of a common tradition* that could have been practiced as easily by a trade guild as by a religious society. Furthermore, *the same basic patterns were present whether the meal was designated as "sacred" or "secular."* "On the one hand, there was a religious component to every 'secular' meal. On the other hand, every 'sacred' banquet was also a social occasion."[1]

BANQUET CUSTOMS IN THE ANCIENT WORLD

POSTURES. For ordinary meals in the part of the world that Jesus came from, even today it is the normal custom to eat while sitting on the ground or on a cushion. The meal is placed on a very low table in the midst of the guests and is presented in a common dish from which all help themselves with their fingers; hence the practice of washing hands before and after a meal.[2] (Reclining on benches or sitting on chairs around a fairly high table *may* have been the custom among the more affluent.[3])

Although the Greeks, Romans and Jews originally had in common the custom of *sitting* at meals, as early as the eighth century BCE in the Eastern Mediterranean region the custom of *reclining* at meals had developed.[4] Jewish data from the New Testament period shows that reclining was the normal posture for formal meals, usually in the evening (such as the Passover liturgy).[5] In the gospels, whenever a posture is indicated for the meals of Jesus, it is always the posture of *reclining.* It was also the custom of certain "closed societies," such as the adherents of Mithras.[6] Couches were furnished in dining rooms so that guests could recline.

RANKING GUESTS AT TABLE.   There was always a ranking associated with the arrangement of these couches. "Thus, each guest would be placed according to his status in relation to that of the other guests. Ranking the guests appropriately could be a tricky procedure for the hosts, and embarrassing situations and social gaffes are commonplace in the literature."[7] (Recall the parable in Luke 14: 7–11.)

> Normally, the ranking order started at the highest position and continued around the room to the right to the lowest position. It was also customary for diners to share couches. . . . The vase paintings show diners reclining on their left sides and eating with their right hands.[8]

In both John 13:23 (the beloved disciple reclined next to Jesus) and Luke 16:22 (Lazarus in the bosom of Abraham), the reference is to an individual who reclines at the right of the host or guest of honor and thus has an honored position at the table.

WASHING.   "It was customary for the household servant to wash the feet of the guests before they reclined, as indicated, for example, in Plato's *Symposium.*"[9] In the New Testament, we see the "sinful" woman washing Jesus' feet as he reclined at the house of Simon the Pharisee (Luke 7:44). And, of course, we see Jesus himself washing the feet of his disciples (John 13:1–11). Washing the hands was also a normal part of Greco-Roman banquet customs. In Judaism, this custom was elevated to a religious ritual.[10]

THE IDEOLOGY OF BANQUETS

As Mary Douglas has noted, meals are not simply about food; they are also (and even more fundamentally) about social relations:

> If food is treated as a code, the messages it encodes will be found in the pattern of social relations being expressed. The message is about different degrees of hierarchy, inclusion and exclusion, boundaries and transactions across the boundaries. Like sex, the taking of food has a social component, as well as a biological one.[11]

There can be little doubt that in the typical practices of the Greco-Roman world, meals represented a "social code" that expressed patterns of social relations.[12] Meals functioned to define groups and their values—as well as relations among group members—by "incarnating" 1) social bonding, 2) social obligation, 3) social stratification and 4) social equality.

SOCIAL BONDING. The meal (in Greco-Roman as in other societies) created special ties among the diners. It became the primary means for celebrating and enhancing community bonds and became the chief social activity of various groups of comrades and acquaintances. The meal defined boundaries among the various social groups and associations and defined the meaning of "friendship." (Friends were, above all, those who shared the same table; recall how Jesus' practice of dining with sinners and tax collectors caused his opponents to call him a "friend" of such people.)

SOCIAL OBLIGATION. The special tie created among diners at a common table led, in turn, to "an ethical obligation of each to the other."[13] What we moderns call "etiquette" would have been considered, in the Greco-Roman world, "a significant category of social ethics." There developed, indeed, a broad tradition of philosophical discussion about "symposium laws," in which "etiquette was included under important ethical categories such as 'friendship,' 'love,' 'joy,' or 'pleasure.' "[14] Thus, *etiquette* (which includes all those social rules that govern posture, physical attitude, etc.) was seen as the incarnation of *ethics.*

In these discussions, ethics were defined not as individual but as group values. That was considered "ethical" which served the goal of friendship or the pleasure of the group *as a*

49

whole. These discussions thus focused on the ways behavior is defined to serve the common good. For example, quarreling and abusive talk were banned from the table *because they failed to serve the goal of "good cheer" among the diners.* Similarly, factional cliques were forbidden because they offended the goal of *solidarity among the diners* (see 1 Corinthians 11:17–34).

SOCIAL STRATIFICATION. A table in the ancient world was crisscrossed by both visible and invisible boundaries: *Reclining was a posture that itself indicated social rank,* since traditionally, to recline at table was reserved to males who were free citizens. Reclining was forbidden to women, children and slaves. However, in Roman times, the older discipline that governed reclining began to be relaxed as women began to recline among the men. Even so, the older "social code" survived; if a banquet at which women were present became so crowded that there was no more room for a late-arriving male guest to recline, it was considered insulting and "womanish" to *sit* at the table. The late-comer would rather recline on the floor than "sit" at table.[15] "The same 'social code' is evidently being addressed in the Jewish Passover liturgy found in the Mishnah, for it specified that even the poor are to 'recline' at this meal: 'And even the poorest Israelite should not eat until he reclines at this table.' "[16]

The egalitarian aspects of Jesus' meal practice seem to have shared at least some of the Passover traditions of Israel. At Passover, social rank was ignored or subverted so that "even the poorest" could recline during this festival of Israel's freedom. Perhaps one could say that Jesus extended "Passover egalitarianism" to all human situations of meal-and-table sharing. In this sense, Jesus might be said to have radically "equalized the table," making it a place where the presence of the "greatest" would not in any way diminish or threaten the participation of the "least"—making it a place where all without distinction are forever welcome.

It was considered *ethical* (a sign of the "good order" that was supposed to characterize banquets) in the Greco-Roman world to recognize a person's social status at table. This could be done in a variety of ways: *placement* at table; *quality* and *quantity of the food* served to the person. Sometimes these means were used to designate rank within a social organization: ". . . club officers would be designated

assigned places at table and special portions in the distri-
bution of meat. So also the placement of individuals at
the communal meals of the Essenes at Qumran was specified according to their rank in the community.[17]

There is, then, clear evidence from the time of Jesus (for
example, from Qumran) that religious meals included not
only "worship of God" and "communion among the diners" but also gestures and postures marking differences of
social rank and hierarchical status. One must ask, however,
whether such social ranking within the context of a religious meal agrees either with Jesus' meal practice or with
his egalitarian message about the reign of God. The mere
fact that religious customs reflecting social ranking at
meals existed in Jesus' time is not, in itself, sufficient warrant to import such a practice into the meals of Christians
or to continue that practice if (in fact) it has already infil-
trated the Christian assembly. Moreover, there is good reason to believe that Jesus rejected the "Essene option" as
the best way to enter into—and nourish—a relationship
with God. The "Jesus movement" was neither a movement
of "eremitical withdrawal" from ordinary social and politi-
cal life nor a segregation of the "religious elite" from the
"unwashed mass of sinners." Jesus appears to have repudi-
ated such a religious and racial apartheid. Indeed, Jesus
threw in his lot with sinners, eating with them, associating
with them and taking upon himself their opprobrium and
despised status.

SOCIAL EQUALITY.   In spite of their inevitable links with
social ranking and stratification, meals in the Greco-Roman
world could also function as signs of social equality.[18]

> A reference in Plutarch [Table Talk 616C–F] is especially
> instructive. He refers to a banquet where the group agreed to
> forego the normal ranking at table and to recline where
> each individual diner wished. In the accompanying conver-
> sation, such equality at the meal is argued for as an inherent
> aspect of banquet 'friendship.' *According to this line of argu-*
> *ment, the diners should leave behind the divisive social*
> *rankings of outer society and in effect form a new society*
> *with new social rules when they entered the door of the*
> *dining chamber.*[19]

One should note, however, that almost in the same breath,
Plutarch argues for the orderliness of ranking and against
the anarchy that results from its abolition.

In the Greco-Roman world, meals often communicated ambiguous messages of both equality and hierarchy—and kept these messages in constant tension. Even groups that promoted equality manifested this ambiguity in their meal customs. Thus, while at the tables of the Therapeutae (as described by Philo) there were no slaves, and the women reclined as did the men (albeit in a separate section of the room), even here there was ranking according to seniority in the community.[20]

There was nothing especially distinctive about the Christian custom of assembling for meals. Every group in the ancient world celebrated communal meals. It is entirely predictable that Christians would have done the same thing—but the interpretations of these meals differed considerably.

THE NEW TESTAMENT BANQUET: IMPROVISATIONS ON A THEME

LAST SUPPER TRADITION. At least four different versions of the Last Supper tradition are found in the New Testament. Three of these (Paul [1 Corinthians 11:23–26], Mark [14:22–25], and Luke [22:15–20]) place their emphasis on the "eucharistic sayings" of Jesus. The fourth (John 13:1–11) ignores these sayings altogether, emphasizing instead the ritual of the footwashing at the meal.

Christians often forget that at least one of the principal theologies of the eucharist in the New Testament (namely, that contained in John) is expressed entirely in terms of ritual gesture and posture without attention either to an "institution narrative" or a "dominical command" to repeat the bread-and-wine procedures. The "command to repeat" in John is actually a command about mutual service—not a command to repeat "words of Jesus" or even to repeat this "last meal" of Jesus with his friends.

It is virtually impossible to interpret all four versions in the New Testament texts as either "references to a historical event" or references to a "single liturgical tradition" common to all early Christians.[21] Not only does the New Testament give us various "versions" of Jesus' "sayings at the supper," it also points to a variety of models for the kind of focus the meal might have had. Was it a "memorial meal," on the model of a Greco-Roman "funerary banquet" ("As often as you do this, you proclaim the Lord's death")? Was it a "covenant meal," structured on the model of a "club banquet" ("This cup is the new covenant in my blood")? Or was it a meal dominated by the theme of the "eschatological banquet" ("I shall not drink again of the fruit of the vine")?

The text tradition of Jesus' "eucharistic words" does not provide a liturgical script (as do *Didache* 9 and 10). Instead, it provides a model of "interpretation(s)" attached to actions (taking, blessing, breaking, sharing). The Last Supper tradition, moreover, does not exhaust all the meal traditions and practices known to the ancient church.

> [T]here are other meal traditions in the early church that refer neither to the Last Supper tradition nor to the idea that the meal is a commemoration of the death of Jesus. . . . Our data does not witness to a single origin or singular meaning for early Christian meals. Rather, the meal apparently came to exist as a center of communal self-identity based on its own inherent meaning in the culture. It needed no further justification.[22]

THE "MEAL MINISTRY" OF JESUS AND THE MEALS OF THE EARLY CHRISTIANS.

Norman Perrin argued that the New Testament traditions about Jesus' meal practices are historical (i.e. are really descriptions of Jesus' historical life and ministry). Even if these traditions are not entirely accurate, there is little doubt that "Jesus spent a lot of time at banquets."[23] This in itself would not have been particularly unusual in the ancient Greco-Roman world, where shared meals were a normal part of life and a common way for people of similar interests and occupations to associate.

In addition, it is quite probable "that Jesus not only attended banquets, but also, in a style consistent with symposium tradition, taught at them as well. This correlates with the fact that the sayings of Jesus contain many allusions to the motif of a meal."[24] The connection between meal and teaching was known in both Judaism[25] and Greco-Roman philosophical tradition:[26] "What we derive from the historical Jesus data is not the establishment of a specific meal tradition but the possible utilization of ordinary meal tradition as part of a larger teaching process."[27]

53

The charges levelled against Jesus in the New Testament ("Behold . . . a friend of sinners, a glutton and drunkard") may actually reflect critiques of the early Christian community.[28] The charge is that of engaging in sloppy dining habits. This probably meant that, though the community still located itself within the context of synagogue social structure, it had begun to practice some kind of separate table fellowship (suggesting a separate social identity) that placed it at odds with other Jews. In particular, the meals were shockingly open to "outsiders," as the community experimented with the normal boundaries of their social setting.

As "boundary markers" (for both "normal" Jews and for the emerging "Jesus movement" community), *meals function as increasingly strong indicators of social identity.*

> Indeed, since this community originally had its primary social and religious identity in the social setting of the synagogue, its gathering to celebrate a separate communal meal may have been the primary way in which it began to develop a separate community identity. The process whereby this text [about Jesus as drunkard and glutton] came to be formed, written down, and preserved is a record of its progress toward an identity as a completely separate community defined at least partially by its communal meals.[29]

Note, then, that one may see here an important link between the evolution of the Christian community's meal tradition and its emergence as a separately identified religious group (a church). This linkage can be seen in a four-stage process. In the first stage, Christians are part of the synagogue but begin to gather for separate meals, for festive banquets (a typical practice of clubs and associations in the Greco-Roman world). In the second stage, the meals among Christians become occasions for testing and transgressing the boundaries of their customary "social set" (the social world of Jewish synagogue life). The third stage occurs when the Christian meals begin to function as barometers of an emerging community identity that is new and distinctive. Finally, during the fourth stage, Christians "quit going to church"—that is, they abandon the social and religious life of the synagogue altogether (or are "pushed out," or some combination of the two)—and become a completely separate community defined at least partially by its communal meals. In short, meals become both the focus of the "Jesus movement" community's estrangement from the synagogue and the nucleus of its developing identity as a sectarian group.

Note, however, that while the meal tradition may have served as a focus for separating Christians from the synagogue, we do not have evidence that the meal is being used as a basis for creating boundaries *within* the Christian group (that is, based on distinctions between "higher" and "lower" degrees of membership, "clergy" and "laity" or a ranking that favors "leaders" over "followers").

PAUL AND THE MEALS AT ANTIOCH

Galatians 2:11–14 already seems to assume both that communal meals are a regular part of the worship activity among the early Christian communities and that these meals were seen as carrying considerable theological weight.

> The form and interpretation of the Christian meal at Antioch appears to be analogous to that of the banquet of any ancient group or club. The meal is functioning as a boundary marker, defining the special identity of this group. The theme of social bonding is especially strong. It is quite likely as well that further worship activities of the community took place at the table.[30]

The source of conflict at Antioch seems to have been both racial and religious. A group from the Jerusalem church (comprised of Jews who still followed the dietary laws) refused to eat with "the Gentiles" in Antioch—although Paul, Barnabas and other Jews at Antioch seem not to have thought it necessary to follow the dietary laws and did not yet think of themselves as "reprobates" cut off from Judaism. In fact, there was a great deal of diversity about dietary regulations in first-century Judaism. The Pharisees had redefined the traditional dietary laws to refer not just to the temple, which was the normal view, but also to the daily table. And the Pharisees, after all, represented a minority view at this juncture. There would have been many Jews in Jesus' time who did not feel obliged to apply these dietary laws to their daily lives and who would have felt comfortable eating with Gentiles. Still there was one hitch. Since Gentiles were considered "idolaters," and since therefore all their foods were potentially "unclean" by having been offered to idols, a Jew might well hesitate to eat at a Gentile table. This would represent a source of dietary restriction different from the tradition promoted by the Pharisees.

From the report in Galatians 2:11–14, one can see that the meal of the Christians in Antioch was being given several different interpretations. Jewish Christians from Jerusalem saw the meal as defining their solidarity with a specific aspect of Jewish tradition. The dietary laws were interpreted in a way that drew boundaries not only between them and the non-Jewish world but also between them and the rest of their fellow Jews. In short, this was a highly sectarian view of the meal. Neither Paul nor Peter, nor any of the other Hellenistic Jews at Antioch, subscribed to this view—although it seems that Peter, when dining with the Jerusalem group, accepted their customs (as he accepted the customs of the Christians at Antioch when he dined with them). The meeting of the two groups at Antioch, however, forced people like Peter to make a choice. Peter decided to dine with the visitors from Jerusalem—thereby prompting a severe rebuke from Paul, who had a different vision of the significance of the meal. Paul saw the communal meal as "a highly effective, fundamental means for drawing boundaries and establishing community identity."[31] When the Jerusalem group refused to eat with the Antioch group, Paul saw this as a sign of boundaries being drawn *within* the community. Paul was a strong believer in the unitive power of liturgy; and he saw the Jerusalem group's behavior as an act of ritual exclusion. So for Paul, the situation was not simply a matter of "tolerating diverse customs" but a matter of fundamental theology.

> For [Paul], liturgy had to cohere with theology. The theology that all espoused stated that "justification" was through "faith in Jesus Christ" for both Jews and Gentiles (Galatians 3:15–16). The liturgy as they had just practiced it belied that theology. Liturgically, they had proclaimed two gospels, not one. For Paul, then, the primary function of the meal was community formation, and to gather for two meals would mean in effect that there were two communities, not one.[32]

Peter's view (and apparently that of Barnabas) differed from Paul's in that while Peter probably would have agreed that the meal had high value for community formation, it was not necessary to have a single liturgy into which all variations would be absorbed.

> One can therefore speculate that, whereas Paul defined the effectiveness of liturgy in terms of its coherence with

a larger theological picture, Peter defined it in terms of its coherence with the needs and experiences of individual groups. . . . [I]t is a view that takes . . . an equally strong reliance on the social code of ancient meals but looks at the social bonding function of the meal from a local rather than global perspective. Consequently, Peter's view can be seen as one that sees liturgy as a way to recognize and affirm diversity in the group.[33]

THE "LORD'S SUPPER" AT CORINTH

At Corinth (as at Antioch) the problems surrounding the community meal seem, in Paul's view, to have stemmed from a tendency to eat separately (see 1 Corinthians 11:20–21). The solution? Wait for one another and, when all have gathered, eat together (see 1 Corinthians 11:33–34). The theological motive? The community is the Lord's "body"— and hence as one body, the community must remain united in its banquet (see 1 Corinthians 11:23–32).

The central meaning of meal here (as at Antioch) is its function in *ritualizing social bonding for the community.* The primary symbol of this bonding is eating together. This ritual process is disrupted if rival groups are allowed to separate for the meal (as at Antioch) or if factions form within the group for whatever reason—perhaps because of socio-economic differences in the community (as at Corinth) and conflicts between rich and poor. *"The act of gathering in the same place at the same time has ritual force."* Social bonding is also signified by the act of sharing food.

> Here the symbolism is that the sharing of bread together serves to ritualize the bonds that make them into a community or 'body.' It is a concept that is derived from meal tradition. Plutarch, for example, refers to the same idea in connection with the sharing of wine. When Paul utilizes the traditional equation of the bread with 'body' [see 1 Corinthians 11:24] as the center of his specific interpretation, he is apparently referring to the ritual enactment of this meaning in the act of sharing bread.[34]

Paul is thus making heavy use of the meal tradition as a dominant "social code" within his culture. Indeed, he ascribes such theological weight to the meal that it becomes, for him, a proclamation of the Lord's death. For Paul, the Lord's death is proclaimed not so much in word as it is in liturgical witness.

CONCLUSIONS

■ In Jesus' own life and ministry, the meal tradition—
whatever it may have signified—almost certainly was not
related to community formation. Jesus did not envision the
establishment of yet another religious community or religious movement. He envisioned, instead, the arrival of
God's reign in the present moment of human existence as
a reality available to all who have "eyes to see" and "ears
to hear." In this light, it seems that his meal ministry
was the effective proclamation and *realization* of the radical
in-breaking of the reign of God.

■ In the meals of the earliest Christians (as exemplified, for
instance, in the document Q), a sense of community formation does develop:

> Here, an increasing estrangement from the Jewish commu-
> nity of which they were a part caused them to develop
> a heightened sense for the way in which a meal defines
> boundaries. In this case both inclusion and exclusion were
> given special emphasis as meal ideology was utilized to
> give cohesion and self-identity to the group as well as to
> provide ways to legitimate the inclusion of controversial
> new members.[35]

■ The tradition about the "Last Supper" is not one tradition, but many. One set of traditions emphasizes formulaic
benedictions by Jesus over the bread and wine. Another set
emphasizes the link between the meal and Jesus' death
(see 1 Corinthians 11:26–27). Still another emphasizes neither bread and wine nor death but the act of humble service in footwashing.

■ The Pauline documents reveal several distinct meal
traditions. In the controversy at Antioch, for instance, at
least *three different positions or interpretations* are alluded
to: Paul's own (liturgy must cohere with theology; universal liturgical practice must accord with universal theological conviction); that of Peter (local diversity and variation
represents no threat to real unity); and that (implied) of
James and the Jerusalem party (as a code for social boundaries, the meal must reflect differences not only between
Jews and non-Jews, but even within the community
between Jewish Christians and Hellenistic Christians).

■ Wherever the communal meal was practiced, the community recognized the meal's function as one of defining

boundaries and bonding the members together. In adapting the meal tradition, the various communities responded to specific aspects of their own social situations and were doing so using a ritual 'language' that was especially meaningful in their culture.[36]

■ Although the celebration of the eucharist was sooner or later separated from the communal meal tradition, the sociological and theological significance of the meal tradition and its interpretations did have implications for the way the eucharist was understood and celebrated throughout the first millennium.

The purpose of the next chapter is to trace the development of postures that were assumed after the eucharist and the meal were considered distinct entities, with a focus on the posture assumed during the eucharistic prayer.

ENDNOTES

1. Dennis Smith and Hal Taussig, *Many Tables: The Eucharist in the New Testament and Liturgy Today* (Philadelphia: Trinity Press International, 1990), 21–22.

2. Helene Lubienska de Lenval, *The Whole Man at Worship: The Actions of Man before God,* trans. by Rachel Attwater (New York: Desclee Company, 1961), 28ff. "For the meal at a festival the candlesticks and spare dishes of food were placed on a high, square piece of furniture, perhaps the ancestor of the many square altars of Christian times, and the company sometimes stood around this and sometimes sat on the ground around the low table. From the beginning, the Breaking of Bread has always and everywhere been celebrated standing."

3. Lubienska de Lenval, 28.

4. See, e.g., Amos 6:4–7. Since Greeks, Romans and Jews interacted thorughout this period of history, it is not surprising that common conventions surrounding meals (including the custom of reclining) developed and persisted.

5. This is the tradition represented in the Mishnah for the Passover liturgy. See *Mishnah Pesachim* 10.1

6. As Roman excavations have shown. See Lubienska de Lenval, 28.

7. Smith and Taussig, *Many Tables,* 24.

8. Ibid., 24.

9. Ibid., 25.

10. See *Mishnah Hagigah* 2.5; see also Mark 7:3, where the hand-washing is a point of dispute between Jesus and the Pharisees.

11. M. Douglas, "Deciphering a Meal," *Daedalus* 101 (1972): 61.

12. See Smith and Taussig, 30–31.

13. Ibid., 31.

14. Ibid.

15. See ibid., 32–33.

16. Ibid., 33.

17. Ibid.

18. Such "banquets among *equals*" seem to have been known already in Homer (*Iliad* 1.468, 602; 2.431, etc.).

19. Smith and Taussig, 34.

20. See ibid., 34.

21. Ibid., 40. "The tradition does not support the view that the Last Supper tradition derives from any hypothetical single original event, whether that event be located in the life of Jesus or in the life of the early church" (41).

22. Ibid., 43.

23. Ibid., 47. For Perrin's position, see his *Rediscovering the Teaching of Jesus.*

24. Ibid.

25. For example, the sage at table discussing the law in Sirach 9:14–15 and *Mishnah Abot* 3.3.

26. The Cynic philosopher was perhaps the closest Greek counterpart to the tradition of the Hebrew wisdom sage.

27. Smith and Taussig, 48.

28. Ibid., 48–49.

29. Ibid.

30. Ibid., 59–60.

31. Ibid., 62.

32. Ibid.

33. Ibid., 62–63.

34. Ibid., 65.

35. Ibid., 67.

36. Ibid., 69.

CHAPTER FOUR OUTLINE

I. Standing: *Orans*

II. Standing: *Inclinans*

III. *Genua flectens*

    A. Non-participants: fasts and ferias

    B. Worship of the holy eucharist
        1. Elevation and gestures of adoration
        2. Eucharistic worship vs. tradition
        3. Distinctions disappear

    C. Priestly genuflections

    D. The *Ordo* of Burchard and the Missal of 1570

    E. The liturgical movement and the reforms of Vatican II
        1. Priest's genuflections reduced
        2. *General Instruction of the Roman Missal,* no. 21
        3. The bishops' decision: 1969
        4. Contemporary practice

IV. Conclusions

POSTURE DURING THE EUCHARISTIC PRAYER | 4

As we saw in Chapter Three, the postures assumed in the context of a ritual meal had much to say about the social status and function of those present. One thing that is absolutely clear from the New Testament is the radical equality of table fellowship in the community of the disciples. If anything, the traditional roles of servant and served were reversed. Those who had any claim to leadership in the community were soon designated by the titles of overseers *(episcopoi)* and table-waiters *(diakonoi)*. Clearly, servanthood and service *(diakonia)* were at the heart of the Christian community.

When eventually the eucharist was celebrated apart from the community's meals, the ideal of equality was not abandoned, even as the roles of *episcopoi* and *diakonoi* evolved and the order of *presbyteroi* emerged. All the early evidence indicates that as tables and couches for reclining were replaced with a single altar/table, the entire community assumed the standing posture of servants—servants at prayer.

STANDING: ORANS

The earliest evidence regarding the posture assumed by Christians during the eucharistic prayer indicates standing with arms outstretched.[1] As has already been noted, standing with uplifted hands and with eyes fixed in the direction of the rising sun was the ordinary posture of prayer among most ancient peoples,[2] just as reclining was the ordinary posture for festive meals. This posture of prayer was continued by all Christians, in common and in private, with this variant: They saw in the rising sun an image of the Risen Christ.[3]

The figure of the *orant* or *orantes* is well attested in early Christian iconography,[4] and there is little doubt that this posture was assumed by all the faithful during the presidential prayers, including the anaphora.[5] In speaking of the appropriateness of praying for the dead, John Chrysostom refers to the entire assembly standing with arms outstretched during the anaphora:

> When the whole people together with the priestly assembly stands with hands outstretched, at the awe-inspiring sacrifice, how can we fail to please God by praying for the dead.[6]

In its origin, the great eucharistic prayer was not distinguished from other presidential prayers by any special signs of veneration or by any special gestures.[7] When it was improvised, as attested to in the third-century *Apostolic Tradition* of Hippolytus, the anaphora was solemnly proclaimed by the presiding minster, who was charged to ensure that the words he used were "orthodox" (literally, "correct praise"). When the Roman Canon became more or less fixed in the sixth century, the ancient posture for prayer was still assumed by the entire assembly—the *circumadstantes*, who are mentioned in the text of the prayer.[8]

STANDING: INCLINANS

In the earliest liturgical books of the West, there was one exception to the rule that the assembly assumed the motions and deportment of the presiding bishop or presbyter: the blessing. For blessings, the assembly was "notified" that its posture was to be different from that of the presider by a diaconal command: *Humiliate capita vestra Deo* [Bow down your heads before God]. The bishop then turned to the assembly and invoked a blessing over their bowed heads. The early books presume that unless certain members of the assembly were explicitly ordered to assume a particular posture for whatever reason, the entire assembly would assume the same bodily posture as the presiding minister.[9]

In the course of the seventh and eighth centuries, the bow of the head became more and more a sign of humility in the sight of God and was assumed no longer for blessings alone but for all the presidential prayers.[10] *Ordo Romanus Primus (Ordo I)*, the oldest surviving description of the Roman Mass (c. 700), indicates that all those present stood upright for the preface; but from the beginning of the Sanctus to the end of the canon, they stood with heads bowed. The bishop alone stood upright and "entered into the canon." Those who had specific tasks during the canon, such as the subdeacons and the archdeacon, stood upright at appropriate times. But all the others, even the suburban bishops and titular presbyters, were to remain *inclinantes.*[11]

Ordo Romanus Primus is silent regarding the posture of the faithful during the canon. But because the document very explicitly describes when the members of the the assembly are to do anything at all—such as bringing forward the gifts to various places during the *offertorium* or where to stand and from whom to receive communion (both species) —it is safest to presume that they, like the various orders of clergy present, stood with bowed heads.

This same posture was still considered normative for the eucharistic prayer as late as the tenth and eleventh centuries, when the liturgies and customs of the Cluniac Benedictines and Cistercians were compiled. In nearly all their editions—some as late as the seventeenth and eighteenth centuries—the sacramentaries and customaries of these orders direct the entire community to remain standing but inclined during the canon, except on penitential days, when they take to their knees.[12] Long after kneeling or prostrating for the consecration became widespread, "the canons of various cathedral churches continued to follow their age-old practice of bowing. At Chartres this was done as late as the eighteenth century."[13]

The medieval commentaries on the Mass provide more evidence for this posture as well as the earliest indication that the presider is also to bow at various points during the canon.[14] The particulars of the allegorical interpretations are not as important as the fact that commentators from Amalarius in the early ninth century to Durandus at the end

65

of the thirteenth attest to the same *inclinans* we first saw described in *Ordo Romanus Primus*. At the same time, not one of them offers an interpretation for kneeling, or even genuflecting, during the canon. For this entire period, kneeling was not considered an official posture for the eucharistic prayer.

GENUA FLECTENS

NON-PARTICIPANTS: FASTS AND FERIAS. In spite of the lack of witnesses among the medieval commentators, it is possible that, at *certain* Masses as early as the eighth or ninth century, some of those in attendance took to their knees during the canon instead of inclining their heads. The earliest evidence for the practice is found in *Ordo Romanus Quartus (Ordo IV)*, one of a collection of *ordines* compiled by a reform-minded Frankish scribe in the late eighth century.[15] After describing a special form of concelebration for major solemnities, the document adds a note about other days:

> And if the day is not a solemnity, after the chalice is placed on the altar (at the offertory), the presbyters return to the presbyterium (in the apse) and the other clergy return to their places in front of the platform; and if it happens to be Sunday, the presbyters stand with heads bowed, but if it is an ordinary day, they kneel when they begin the Sanctus.
>
> The acolytes, with linens (over their shoulders) come and stand to the left and right behind the deacons. One of them, covered with a linen decorated with a silk cross, stands first holding the paten in front of his chest; some others stand holding chalices and cruets, and the rest holding the *saccula* [small linen bags for holding the eucharistic bread].
>
> And when [during the concluding doxology] the pontiff comes to *omnis honor et gloria* [*all glory and honor is yours, almighty Father*], he raises two of the oblata while the deacon takes the chalice and raises it a little until the pontiff says, "*Per omnia saecula saeculorum* [*for ever and ever*]." Then the deacons and the priests rise from prayer.[16]

The fact that this *ordo* has been preserved in only one manuscript, plus the lack of any corroborative evidence in the writings of the medieval commentators, may indicate that either the *ordo* was never actually followed or that the practice of kneeling for the canon on ordinary days was not very widespread. Even if the practice was known, it is clear from *Ordo IV* that all stood for the eucharistic prayer

on feasts and Sundays and that the attending presbyters,
deacons and schola (and faithful), who unlike the acolytes
were not "exercising their liturgical roles" on these ordinary days, would all be on their knees. In other words, the
ordo does not connect kneeling with the canon *per se*
but rather with the rank of the day and whether or not one
is exercising the fullness of one's liturgical ministry.

The next evidence for a posture that differs from standing
inclinans during the canon is the mid-twelfth century customary of the canons of the Lateran basilica:

> On Sundays and on feasts that have nine lessons [at matins],
> from [I] vespers to [II] vespers we do not pray prostrate
> but stand and bow. On feasts of three lessons, we pray pros-
> trate in the evening. At Mass on fast days, namely during
> Lent and throughout the year, except during Pentecost
> [Eastertide] and on feast days when it is not permitted, we
> pray prostrate from after the Sanctus until *per omnia saec-
> ula saeculorum* [*for ever and ever*] is said right before the
> Agnus Dei.[17]

This regulation was for the community, not the ministers.
Once again, the differences in posture were determined by
the liturgical calendar, and recalling that on fast days no
one but the principal ministers received communion,[18] this
difference in posture was assumed by those who were not
full participants in the eucharistic celebration but were
present "for prayer."

In other words, on Sundays and feastdays—when the eucharist was to be the fullest expression of the local church
at prayer—all stood in their respective "orders" and all
shared the common postures. On fast days and "ordinary"
days—originally non-eucharistic days that did not require
the presence and participation of the entire local church—
the celebration of a private eucharist did not include everyone; those "in attendance" tended to be worshipful spec-
tators rather than full participants as on the "obligatory"
eucharistic days. Their difference in posture was, at least
in part, an expression of their separation from the liturgical
actio. They were concerned with the posture for praying,
not for the canon.

WORSHIP OF THE HOLY EUCHARIST. Although the
posture of the faithful on Sundays and festivals was not
officially altered between the ninth and twelfth centuries,

the same era saw the rise of allegorical interpretations of the Mass, the silent recitation of the canon, a marked decrease in the frequency of communion, removal of the cup from the laity, a drastic increase in the number of private masses and a series of debates regarding the real presence of Christ in the Bread and Wine.[19] During the same period, there was also an increase in the popularity of eucharistic miracle stories, which helped to engender and may have been sparked by the theological controversies.

Attention had shifted away from the liturgy as an action of the entire Body of Christ, and away from communion as the ratification of that action, to liturgy as a dramatic representation of the life of Christ and a theophany that inspires wonder and awe. One manifestation of this shift was the addition of several new gestures, such as those done in imitation of Jesus' actions at the Last Supper: Some priests began to pick up the host at the words *accepit panem* [*he took bread*] and to bless it with a sign of the cross.[20] The consciousness of the canon as the great prayer of thanksgiving for what God has done for us in Christ had finally given way to allegorical interpretation: The priest was no longer pronouncing the thankful praise of the entire church as much as he was performing a dramatic re-presentation of the Last Supper.

Elevation and Gestures of Adoration. Throughout the twelfth century, there were disagreements concerning the exact moment of consecration: Do all the words need to be said before any change happens? Or is the bread consecrated as soon as the priest says *"Hoc est enim corpus meum* [*This is my body*]"? The question was not without pastoral ramifications, since ordinary Christians—who barely presumed to receive communion anymore and neither heard nor understood the words of the canon—were worshiping the host as soon as the priest lifted it from the altar. Most theologians argued that such worship was material idolatry if it occurred before the actual words of Christ were spoken.[21]

Consequently, sometime between 1205 and 1210, a collection of synodal decrees was published at Paris to deal with this and other questions of eucharistic doctrine and liturgical practice.[22] Some of its decisions were to affect liturgical practice for centuries, including the following:

> In the canon of the Mass, when they begin the words, *Qui pridie . . . [The day before . . .]*, presbyters are ordered not to elevate the host immediately so that it may be seen by all the people; rather, they are to hold it just in front of their chest until they have said the words *Hoc est enim corpus meum*. At that point, they are to elevate the host so that it may be seen by all.[23]

The Parisian synod did not regulate the posture or gesture of the laity at the time of the elevation, but given the growing eucharistic piety of the time, this visual contact would have been accompanied by acclamations, bowing, kneeling or prostration. In fact, the synod did request that the laity kneel should they happen to see a priest taking communion to the sick or taking Viaticum to the dying:

> The laity are frequently to be admonished that whenever they see the Body of Christ being carried, they should immediately kneel as to their Lord and Creator; and they should pray with hands joined until It has passed by.[24]

In one of his miracle stories, Caesarius of Heisterbach (d. c. 1240) relates that during a visit to Cologne to confirm the election of Otto (c. 1201), Guido of Praeneste, the papal legate, ordered that "at the elevation of the Host all the people in church should kneel at the sound of a bell and remain prostrate until the consecration of the chalice."[25]

Eucharistic Worship vs. Tradition.

The regulation of posture or gesture at the time of the consecration was far from uniform and, as noted above, kneeling was met with great resistance in some places. For the canonists, the question now arose of whether kneeling for the consecration could be done on Sundays and during Eastertide, when kneeling had been expressly forbidden by canon 20 of the Council of Nicea in favor of standing in honor of Christ's resurrection. It seemed to many that kneeling, which for a long time had been interpreted as an expression of contrition of heart[26] and fervent supplication, was inconsistent with the solemn festive character of Sundays and feastdays. Nevertheless—as subsequent decrees indicate—the 1000-year-old prohibition against kneeling on these days found an exception in the new devotion to the eucharist.

This exception soon made its way into some liturgical books. The Franciscan *Ceremonial for Choir and Altar* (c. 1247–1251) directs that on festivals the friars do not prostrate or kneel "except from the elevation of the Lord's

Body" until the beginning of the Lord's Prayer; but on ferial days they prostrate several times with a special act of veneration at the elevation of the host.[27] According to the *Ceremonial of Gregory X* (c. 1275), when the pope attends a Mass at which another is presiding, he kneels for the canon on ferial days but remains standing on festivals, with miter removed, and kneels at the consecration of the bread to "adore the body and blood of Christ."[28] The distinction between ferials and feasts remained in force in the *Ordo missae* of John Burchard (1502): At Masses with singing *(Missae cantate)* on Sundays and feasts, or on any day during the Easter season, participants were to stand for everything except the Confiteor and the consecration itself, when they were to kneel; on ferial days (at masses without singing, *Missae lectae*), they were to kneel for everything except the gospel.[29]

Distinctions Disappear. However, the distinctions between feast and feria, and between *Missa cantata* and *Missa lecta*, were not always preserved in synodal decrees and popular literature. Pronouncements regarding kneeling for the consecration, like the one attributed to Guido of Praeneste, spread like wildfire in some parts of Europe but took much longer to affect popular practice in other places.[30] As late as 1357, John Thornsbey's *Lay Folks Catechism* still makes no mention of kneeling before the sacrament or of kneeling at Mass. But by the end of the same century, John Myrc exhorts pastors to teach this new posture to their parishioners.[31] Another example of the growing insistence on the new posture is John Audelay's *Poem no. 9*, written c. 1426:

> What that thay knele to the sacryng,
> Knelis adoune for one thyng,
> And hold up your hond,
> And thonk the Lord of His grace,
> That al thyng land thou He has,
> Through His swet sond.[32]

In some places, full prostration was encouraged;[33] in others, kneeling with outstretched arms and raising of hands.[34] But simple kneeling seems to have been most common.[35] The choir rules of religious communities that had retained the ancient custom of standing bowed during the canon began to show the influence of this newer attitude: Some indicate kneeling for the institution narrative, while others indicate kneeling at the end of the Sanctus.[36] By the close of the Middle Ages, kneeling to honor the sacrament at the moment of consecration had gained ascendancy over the desire to see it.[37]

PRIESTLY GENUFLECTIONS. One may expect to find contemporary evidence for the introduction of a similar gesture of veneration on the part of the presiding minister; but the earliest is from the fourteenth century, and even then it was done together with the entire community after the Lord's Prayer while a devotional prayer or psalm was prayed.[38] Henry of Hesse (†1397), at the very end of the fourteenth century, speaks disapprovingly of some priests who knelt at the time of the consecration:

> When the words of consecration are completed, they lift the host a palm's height, then rest their raised hand on the altar and kneel; and again they raise the host over their head; and rising from the genuflection, they elevate the sacrament a third time. Such supposed reverence seems to me as though they are playing a game with the sacrament; it is completely lacking in wisdom. Others prolong the elevation of the sacrament so that the people who are standing afar can see better and run off and see the sacrifice elsewhere. Still others, when elevating the host, turn to the left and the right.[39]

Elsewhere, Henry considers the priest's bow (which had appeared only in the thirteenth century)[40] to be sufficient:

> *Qui pridie.* Here, when the *oblata* should be taken, they make the reverence with a bow and with their hands together, which should never be done until the sacrament has been confected; but as soon as the elevation is completed, then should one bow with reverence.[41]

Genuflecting on both knees at the time of the consecration, though it had become customary in some places for those who assisted at the altar,[42] was quite impractical for the presiding minister; and, it must be remembered, genuflection on one knee was not yet recognized as a religious practice.[43] A Missal of Rouen (mid-fifteenth century) is perhaps the earliest favorable witness to a genuflection immediately before the elevation,[44] but there is still no indication of either genuflections or elevations in the first printed edition of the *Missale Romanum* (1474).[45] In fact, of 16 printed editions of the Missal from 1481 to 1561 examined by R. Lippe, only eight include any reference to the elevation of the host or chalice, and only those printed at Paris in 1530 and 1540 mention even a *mediocri inclinatione* on the part of the priest.[46]

THE *ORDO* OF BURCHARD AND THE MISSAL OF 1570.

On the other hand, the 1502 *Ordo missae* of John Burchard, and several subsequent Mass books published at Rome, included the elevations and the genuflections before and after each consecration. These would be incorporated into the Missal of 1570.[47] In spite of the enormous influence of Burchard's *ordo*, the priest's genuflection still took a long time to catch on.[48]

As more and more dioceses and religious orders adopted both the reforms and the liturgical books of the Council of Trent—those who could claim at least 200 years for their own particular rites were free to keep their own books[49]—everyone would eventually be found either kneeling or genuflecting at the consecration, regardless of the season or feast. But, as mentioned already, the same is not true for the rest of the eucharistic prayer. For Burchard and for the *Missale Romanum* of 1570 (whose rubrics governing postures at Mass survived until the *Ordo Missae* of 1969, with a few simplifications in 1960),[50] at sung masses the ministers and those in choir, and by extension the laity,[51] were to stand except for the Confiteor, the consecration, the communion of the faithful and the last blessing. It was only on the ferials of Advent, during Lent and Passiontide, on the Ember days, on the vigils of feasts (1960: outside the Easter season on class II and III feasts) and at Masses for the dead that all were to kneel from the Sanctus until the sign of peace (1960: until the introduction to the Lord's Prayer). But on these days, the assembly also knelt for the prayers before the epistle and for the postcommunion prayers, as well as for the *oratio super populum* in Lent.[52] At "private" or "read" Masses, the people were to kneel for everything except the gospel, even during the Easter season.[53]

In the final analysis, this last rubric explains why Catholics of the last few centuries came to kneel for the eucharistic prayer regardless of fast or feast. Private Masses, though never the ideal, had nonetheless become the norm (a *missa privata* is not the same thing as a *missa solitaria;* it is a "private" Mass, that is, one deprived of full expression because of the lack of ministers, singing, etc.).[54] Burchard's *Ordo*, which was taken almost full scale into the Missal of

1570, was actually entitled *Ordo servandus per Sacerdotem in celebratione Missae sine cantu et sine ministris secundum ritum sancte Romane ecclesie*—that is, *Order to be followed by a priest in the celebration of a Mass without singing and without ministers according to the rite of the holy Roman Church.* The directives for a *missa solemnis* with singing and the ministries of deacon and subdeacon were included in Burchard almost as afterthoughts and rubricated in the *Missale Romanum* as "exceptions." The simpler *missa cantata* (without deacon and subdeacon) barely received any notice at all.[55] The "private" or "read" Mass—the *missa lecta*—was presented as the basic form.

Burchard's *Ordo* and the Missal of 1570 did not affect actual practice in this regard but simply codified the fact that the low mass *(missa lecta, missa privata)* had all but replaced the full, public celebration of the *missa solemnis.* Outside of monasteries, cathedrals and collegiate chapters, the number and the training of required ministers made the full celebration impossible and thus certainly not expected on a daily basis. Besides that, even in cathedrals and monasteries, the establishment of chantries, the stipend system and the number of endowed Masses to be offered for the living and the dead meant that every available presbyter—including those who had no pastoral responsibilities other than saying Mass—had more than enough to fill his quota and so earn his daily Mass-penny.[56]

With such a burden of Masses, it is not surprising that even for Sundays and feastdays the simplest form of the liturgy would be chosen whenever possible or practically necessary. Accordingly, as Jungmann has written so succinctly,

> [I]n the later Middle Ages the rules for posture at low Mass and at Masses conducted with less solemnity were basically the same rules which held outside of feast-days and festal seasons. . . . To retain these regulations regarding kneeling and standing and at the same time to avoid a frequent and, in the last analysis, disturbing change of posture during the short space of a low Mass, some simpler rule had to be devised for low Mass, namely that aside from the Gospel one would kneel all the way through.[57]

Of course, this was never adhered to strictly, especially after provisions were made for people to sit. But the distinction between feast and feria became more and more blurred, because even on Sundays most people attended a low Mass. In the United States, kneeling was characteristic not only

73

at the low Mass but also at the high Mass, except for the gospel and those times when sitting was permitted. This is probably due in part to the fact that the low Mass, the form prevalent at the time, was brought to this country by the earliest Catholic colonists and missionaries. During the eighteenth and nineteenth centuries, even if there was a high Mass celebrated, there were few—if any—churches where a "choir" or cathedral chapter would have been in full view of the assembly to model the differences in posture required by the rubrics. The laity in this country simply did not acquire the liturgical habit.[58]

THE LITURGICAL MOVEMENT AND THE REFORMS OF VATICAN II

The situation remained pretty much the same in Europe as well, until, with the modern liturgical movement, there was a rediscovery of the importance of signs, gestures and postures.[59] There was also a movement to simplify all the rubrics in light of the liturgico-theological research that had been done since Trent.[60] In the early years of the movement, an attempt was made to follow the rubrics exactly, not only from the point of view of the clergy but also from that of the laity. Thus, at Masses with singing, the faithful stood for the chants and remained standing, like the priest, for the official prayers, especially the preface. Then, after some hesitation but still in accord with the choir rubrics for solemn Masses, they stood for the rest of the canon, with the exception of the institution narrative. Finally, there were many who advocated standing throughout the eucharistic prayer.

With no small thanks to the liturgical movement, the Second Vatican Council decreed that

> both texts and rites should be so drawn up that they express more clearly the holy things they signify and the Christian people, as far as possible, are able to understand them with ease and to take part in the rites fully, actively and as befits a community.[61]

The Council called for a revision of the rite of the Mass

> in such a way that the intrinsic nature and purpose of its several parts, as well as the connection between them, may be more clearly manifested, and that devout and active participation by the faithful may be more easily achieved.

74

> For this purpose the rites are to be simplified, due care being taken to preserve their substance. Parts which with the passage of time came to be duplicated, or were added with little advantage, are to be omitted. Other parts which suffered loss through accidents of history are to be restored to the vigor they had in the days of the holy Fathers, as may seem useful or necessary.[62]

PRIEST'S GENUFLECTIONS REDUCED. In the *Second Instruction on the Proper Implementation of the Constitution on the Sacred Liturgy* (1967), the number of priestly genuflections was reduced [63] and the *Ordo Missae* of 1970 preserved only three of these genuflections: after the showing [sic] of the host, after the showing of the chalice and before communion.[64]

However, it is worth noting that in its section on concelebrated Masses, the *General Instruction of the Roman Missal* [GIRM] indicates that the concelebrating priests "look at the eucharistic bread and chalice as these are being shown and afterward bow low"—which means that only the presiding minister genuflects.[65]

GENERAL INSTRUCTION OF THE ROMAN MISSAL, NO. 21. As for the rest of the assembly:

> [I]n all Masses, unless other provision is made, the faithful should stand from the beginning of the entrance song . . . until the end of the Mass. They should sit for the reading(s) before the gospel and responsorial psalm, for the homily, while the gifts are prepared, and after communion if there is a period of silence. They should kneel [*genuflectant*] at the consecration unless prevented by lack of space, large numbers of people present, or some other reasonable cause.[66]

The ancient practice of standing for prayer has thus been restored as the norm, but the thirteenth-century exception (kneeling at the consecration) has nevertheless been maintained. It should be noted that the verb *genuflectere* was translated "genuflect" to indicate the gesture of the priest after he shows the host and chalice, respectively; but it was translated as "kneel" to indicate the posture of the faithful "at the consecration." Strictly speaking, the presiding minister and the faithful could both obey the rubrics by genuflecting together after the showing of the host and the chalice, respectively.

However, this instruction concerning posture also made it clear that

> [t]he conference of bishops may adapt the actions and postures described in the Order of the Roman Mass to the usage of the people, but these adaptations must correspond to the character and meaning of each part of the celebration.[67]

Thus, in actual practice, GIRM no. 21 was interpreted in a variety of ways as soon as it was published:

■ The Bishops' Conferences of Belgium, the Netherlands, France, and the French sector of Canada opted for standing throughout the eucharistic prayer;

■ In Spain and Italy, the bishops accepted no. 21 as provided in the *General Instruction*—i.e., standing throughout except for the consecration;

■ In November of 1969, the American Bishops, like those of the English sector of Canada, opted for kneeling from "after the singing or recitation of the Sanctus until after the 'Amen' of the eucharistic prayer, that is, before the Lord's Prayer."[68]

This American exception to the *General Instruction* maintained continuity with the old choir rubrics for the ferials of Advent, Lent and other fast days,[69] while the GIRM's call for genuflecting "*ad consecrationem*" echoes instead the choir rubric for the sung mass on Sundays and feasts.[70]

THE BISHOPS' DECISION: 1969. Although extensive minutes of the 1969 discussion were not available for consultation, three documents related to that decision do exist: (a) a *Preliminary Inquiry*; (b) *Proposals and Documentation*, actually used and voted on during the meeting; and (c) the report of the Bishops' Committee on the Liturgy, included in the minutes of the meeting.[71]

Issued in August of 1969, the *Preliminary Inquiry* was sent to all the American bishops to provide background on the liturgical matters to be discussed at the November meeting and to solicit initial feedback. With regard to the posture for the eucharistic prayer, the document explained that standing had been restored as a sign of respect, reverence and attention, as is the case during the proclamation of the gospel. The *Inquiry* also noted that the restored posture would help limit the number of changes of posture, that the three new eucharistic prayers were shorter than the Roman Canon, and that common practice in the United States

76

only differed from the revision proposed in GIRM no. 21 precisely with regard to the eucharistic prayer. Finally, the
Inquiry informed the bishops that the Conference did
not have to take action on the issue, since the *General
Instruction* was clear enough, but that it might be prefer-
able to be explicit about posture.

One proposal included in the *Inquiry* was phrased thus:
"That the Directives of the Roman Missal concerning
the posture of the congregation at Mass should be left
unchanged." Of the 140 bishops who responded, 93 were
affirmative, 47 negative. A second proposal in the *Inquiry*
suggested that the kneeling prescribed in GIRM, no. 21
"begin after the singing or recitation of the Sanctus and
end with the 'Amen' of the concluding doxology." To this
proposal, 135 inquiry respondents agreed, 5 disagreed.
Based on the results of this second vote, the first question
had been interpreted by most bishops to mean that the
"Directives of the Roman Missal" did not refer to GIRM,
no. 21 but to the Tridentine rubrics for low Mass.

As a result of the *Inquiry,* the Committee on the Liturgy
drafted *Proposals and Documentation* for use at the actual
meeting in November. This document included a requested
clarification:

> Some inquiries have been received about the reason for
> standing after the elevation. While the Missal provides this
> because of Roman tradition, an additional reason is found
> in the new acclamation after the consecration; the change to
> a standing position helps to emphasize the intention for the
> people to sing or say the acclamation. It also serves to sepa-
> rate the acclamation and show that it is related to the next
> prayer [i.e., the anamnesis] of the priest.

It also included the proposal voted on during the meeting:

> That number 21 of the *General Instruction on the Roman
> Missal* be adapted so that the people kneel during the
> celebration of Mass beginning after the singing or recita-
> tion of the Sanctus until after the Amen of the eucharistic
> prayer, that is, before the Lord's prayer."

The final vote was 184 in favor, 9 opposed.

A *Report of the Liturgy Committee,* included in the minutes
of the Conferences' Meeting in November, 1969, explains
in part the reason behind the American bishops' vote:

> There was some discussion as to whether or not the bishops
> should proceed to vote on the questions as presented. Those

> opposed to action argued that there is need to prepare the
> faithful before implementing any of the called-for changes.
> It was noted that the people are "profoundly disturbed."
> Any new changes should be postponed if possible. In answer
> to these objections, it was asserted that the Holy See itself
> had directed the episcopal conferences to address themselves
> to the matters in question. Delay would lead to dissent
> and dissatisfaction on the part of many. It would give rise to
> serious pastoral problems as well.

Obviously, the American bishops chose to vote on the matter and, as already noted, the vote "spared the people" yet another major change in the celebration of the Mass. Given the tumult and complexity that resulted from mandated changes, this pastoral decision on the part of the bishops is understandable and even commendable. Unfortunately, the "postponement" meant the retention of the old, low Mass posture for the eucharistic prayer in spite of the Council's decision that the *missa cantata* be considered "normative."[72]

CONTEMPORARY PRACTICE. A perceived inconsistency (maintaining the non-participatory posture of the low Mass at the center of a liturgy restored to the entire assembly), along with a poor understanding of the relationship between ecclesiastical and ritual authority, led, in the matter of a few years, to a great diversity of actual practice in the United States and Canada. In most places, people kneel throughout the eucharistic prayer; some kneel from the Sanctus to the memorial acclamation; several places have introduced standing throughout. The resulting confusion has been met with pleas for the reconsideration of the posture during the eucharistic prayer. The Western Liturgical Conference of Canada published their request in January of 1986; in 1991, the Federation of Diocesan Liturgical Commissions recommended that the American bishops take up the issue once again in time for the publication of the revised translation of the Missal of Paul VI. At the same time, several articles were published clamoring for a clamping down on the "irreverence" implied or expressed by standing for the eucharistic prayer.[73]

CONCLUSIONS

■ The earliest posture that was assumed by Christians during the eucharistic prayer was standing with outstretched arms (*orans*).

■ From the eighth to the thirteenth centuries, those fully participating at a liturgy continued to stand for all presidential prayers, including the Canon. Rather than outstretched arms, however, participants stood with heads bowed (*inclinans*); the presider alone stood upright with outstretched arms.

■ In the same period, those who attended Mass on fast days but did not participate fully (that is, the non-communicants), knelt during much of the liturgy.

■ The piety of the thirteenth century brought about a major change. The faithful were admonished to kneel whenever they saw "the Lord's Body." Officially, however, the posture of the assembly continued to be determined by the level of its participation which, in turn, was determined by the rank of the celebration: For Sundays and feasts, at *missa solemnia* or *missa cantata*, full participants were to stand except for the elevation; for penitential days, at *missa privata* or *missa lecta*, those "in attendance" were to kneel throughout except for the gospel.

■ Only from the thirteenth century was the elevation of the host by the priest regulated in the rubrics. A profound bow by the priest after the elevation appeared later in that century, but the earliest favorable witness to a priestly genuflection is from the mid-fifteenth century.

■ For a variety of reasons, the *missa lecta* or Low Mass became the norm even on Sundays and feastdays. Even when the *missa cantata* or *missa solemnia* was celebrated, most assemblies continued to assume the postures of the Low Mass.

■ Vatican II called for a revision of the Mass so that the "intrinsic nature of its several parts, as well as the connection between them, may be more clearly manifested, and that devout and active participation by the faithful may be more easily achieved."

The church is still in the process of heeding that call. It is our hope that this review of the history and theology of postures for prayer will contribute to that process.

ENDNOTES

1. See above, p. 23. The full quote from J. A. Jungmann, regarding the *circumstantes* can be found in MRR, I: 239–240.

2. See above, p. 22, n. 3.

3. MRR, I:239. Indeed all the postures and gestures of prayer that were done in common were done likewise in private. See Robert Taft, *The Liturgy of the Hours in East and West*, 29. Jungmann notes that in Switzerland after 1500 it still was customary for the faithful to pray with arms outstretched from the consecration until communion.

4. See F. Cabrol, H. Leclercq, H. I. Marrou, *Dictionnaire d'archeologie chretienne et de liturgie* [DACL], 15 vols. (Paris: 1907–1973), XIII.

5. Neunheuser, Burkhard, "*Les Gestes de la prière à genoux et de la génuflexion dans les églises de rite romain*," in A. M. Triacca, et. al., eds., *Gestes et Paroles dans les diverses Familles liturgiques*, Conférences Saint-Serge XXIVe Semaine d'Études liturgiques, Paris, 28e Juin–1er Juillet 1977, Biblioteca Ephemerides Liturgicae Subsidia 14 (Rome: Centro Liturgico Vincenziane, 1978), 153.

6. *Homilia III in Philip, IV*; PG 62: col. 204.

7. The oldest manuscripts present the text of the canon to us without any distinction in the writing of the words, and until the high Middle Ages, the only gestures indicated were the stylized signs of the cross made in the course of its proclamation. See OR VII, in M. Andrieu, ed., *Les ordines romani*, II: 253–305.

8. In the most ancient manuscripts, the *circumstantes* are called the *circum adstantes*, cf. A. Ebner, *Quellen und Forschungen zur Geschichte und Kunstgeschichte des Missale Romanum im Mittelalter* (Freiburg, 1896) 405. See also J. Jungmann, MRR, II: 166. It is an unfortunate result of later developments that this term was translated figuratively as "those here present" in the current ICEL translation of the Roman Canon.

9. Other examples are the commands to the catechumens, the *energoumenoi*, the elect, the candidates for orders. See the respective church orders: *Apostolic Tradition, Apostolic Constitutions, Canons of Hippolytus, Testament of the Lord*, etc. See also the *Ordines Romani:* on baptism, OR XI; on holy orders, ORR XXXIV-XXXVI.

10. J. Jungman, MRR I: 239. From Amalarius to Durandus, the bow was interpreted as a sign of reverence and humility before the majesty of God. On other bowings and their interpretations see Rudolf Suntrup, D*ie Bedeutung der liturgischen Gebärden und Bewegungen in lateinischen und deutschen Auslegungen des 9. bis 13. Jahrhunderts.* Münstersche Mittelalter Schriften, Bd. 37. (München: Wilhem Fink Verlag, 1978), 142–153.

11. *Ordo Romanus Primus;* M. Andrieu, ed., *Les ordines romani*, II: 95-96: . . . *stantes erecti usquedum incipiant dicere hymnum angelicum, id est* Sanctus, Sanctus, Sanctus.

Ut autem expleverint, surgit pontifex solus et intrat in canonem; episcopis, vero, diaconi, subdiaconi et presbiteri in presbiterio permanet inclinati. The subdeacons stood erect at *Nobis quoque* and the archdeacon soon after at the *Per quem haec omnia* so that he could assist the bishop in "lifting the chalice" and *oblatae* during the *Per ipsum.*

12. Paul Tirot, "Un *Ordo Missae* monastique: Cluny, Citeaux, la Chartreuse," *Ephemerides Liturgicae* 95 (1981): 44–120; 220–251; reprinted as *Bibliotheca Ephemerides Liturgicae Subsidia* 21 (Rome, 1981).

13. J. Jungmann, MRR, II: 210-211. Other evidence can be found in P. Browe, "L'aggiamento del corpo durante la messa," *Ephemerides Liturgicae* 50 (1936): 402–414, esp. 408. In the Diocese of Basle in 1581 the Canons of St. Ursitz had to be forced to kneel at the consecration with threats of ecclesiastical penalties. For the French cathedrals, see Claude de Vert, *Explications simple,* I (Paris 1706), 238ff.

14. The earliest manuscripts that include rubrical directives for the various bows of the priest date from the tenth century. On the interpretation of these bows and those of the assisting clergy see Suntrup, *Die Bedeutung der liturgischen Gebärden,* 146, n. 24.

15. M. Andrieu, ed., *Les ordines romani,* II: 137–154; This collection of St.Amand describes neither current Roman nor current Gallican practice, but makes use of both in an attempt to reform the Frankish liturgy.

16. During the canon itself, however, the acolytes who held the paten, the ministerial chalices, cruets of water, and linens for carrying the oblata to the presbyters for the fraction, remained standing regardless of the day; M. Andrieu, ed., *Les ordines romani, II:* 163–164.

17. Ludwig Fischer, ed., *Bernhardi cardinales et Lateranensis prioris Ordo officiorum ecclesiae Lateranensis,* Historisches Forschungen und Quellen, 2/3 (München und Friesing: F.P. Datterer, 1916), 29.

18. The canons of the Lateran received communion on Sundays and major feasts; see ibid., pp. 12, 48, 58, 65, 74, 86, and 108. Bernard notes that although one is excommunicated in the East after missing communion on three consecutive Sundays, and both Ambrose and Augustine recommended daily communion, the presbyters and laity of his time were not accustomed to this practice and so the *oratio super populum* was added to the Mass in place of communion; see p. 38. It is worth noting that at Cluny in the eleventh century, no one received communion on fast days except the priest, deacon and subdeacon; see Ulrich, *Consuetudines Cluniacensis,* Bk. II, ch. 30; PL 149: cols. 715–725.

19. For a summary of the major eucharistic controversies, see N. Mitchell, *Cult and Controversy: The Worship of the Eucharist Outside Mass* (New York: Pueblo, 1982), 66–86, 129–151.

20. The signs of the cross that appear as early as the eighth century evolved from the

demonstrative gestures of ancient Roman oratorical style. It was only after they were stylized into signs of the cross that they came to be associated with every form of *benedicere;* see M. Andrieu,ed., *Ordo Romanus VII, in Les Ordines romani, II:* 251–317. There were numerous private prayers, ceremonies and gestures added to the Mass in this era and throughout the Middle Ages, each accompanied by allegorical explanations for the sake of those who could only participate by watching; see J. Jungmann, MRR, I: 92–123.

21. V. L. Kennedy, "The Moment of Consecration and the Elevation of the Host," Mediaeval Studies 6 (1944): 122–150; E. Dumoutet, *Le Desir de Voir l'Hostie* (Paris: Beauchesne, 1926); N. Mitchell, *Cult or Controversy,*151–162.

22. Regarding the date, see V.L. Kennedy, "The Date of the Parisian Decree on the Elevation of the Host," *Mediaeval Studies* 8 (1946): 87–96.

23. J.D. Mansi, ed., *Sacrorum Conciliorum nova et amplissima collectio,* [Mansi] (Florence, 1757–1798), XXII: col. 682. It must be remembered that in spite of this regulation, the elevation was not universally practiced: The Missals of the Papal Court and the Regula Missals of the Franciscans based on them throughout the thirteenth century have no indication of either an elevation or genuflection during the institution narrative. A revision of the curial missal for use at St. Mary Major (Van Dijk dates to 1239) does include the elevation of both host and chalice but still no

genuflections; see Van Dijk-Walker, *The Ordinal of the Papal Court from Innocent III to Boniface VIII and Related Documents.* Spicilegium Friburgenses, 22 (Fribourg: University Press, 1975), 512–513. As late as 1282, the Franciscan Chapter held at Strassbourg still forbad the priest to elevate the chalice or to genuflect at the consecration. See S. J. P. Van Dijk, *Sources of the Roman Liturgy,* (Leiden: Brill, 1963), II: 445.

24. Mansi, XXII: col. 678.

25. *Dialogus Miraculorum Liber IX, Capitulum LI.*

26. Even at the end of the thirteenth century, William Durandus still saw kneeling as an expression of contrition but permits it only for the consecration itself on festivals, Sundays and during the Easter season; *Rationale Divinorum Officiorum* VI 86, 17: *Genua enim in Ecclesia flectere cordis contritionem significat . . .*

27. See S. J. P. Van Dijk, *Sources of the Roman Liturgy,* II: 342.

28. Ceremonial of Gregory X (ca. 1275); M. Dykmans, ed., *Le cérémonial papal de la fin du moyen âge à la renaissance,* vol. 1, Bibliothèque de l'Institut historique belge à Rome 24 (Rome-Brussels, 1977), 208-209.

29. "The faithful who are present at a Mass that is read in this way are to kneel from the beginning until the blessing which is given at the end by the celebrant; but when the gospel is read, they are to stand attentively." [In the missal of Trent (1570), this rubric reads: *Circumstantes autem in Missis*

privatis semper genua flectunt, etiam Tempore Paschali, praeterquam legitur Evangelium. [XVII:2]. . . . At a Mass which is sung, if it is Sunday or a feast or a weekday between Easter and Trinity Sunday, they kneel for the confession, and stand from its ending until it is time for the adoration of the Sacrament— when the celebrant shows It to the people for adoration (= the elevation not the entire canon). After this adoration, they are to stand until the end of Mass. J. W. Legg, ed., *Tracts on the Mass,* Henry Bradshaw Society 27 (London, 1904), 134-135.

30. In a letter to the bishops of England or Ireland in 1219, Honorius III asked for a profound bow at the consecration. Synods at Salisbury (1217) and Oxford (1222) required kneeling; Mansi, XXII: cols. 1119 and 1176. Although the feast of *Corpus Christi* appeared not far from Cologne in Liège in 1246 (and thanks to Jacques Pantaleon, the archdeacon of Liège who became Pope Urban IV, was proclaimed a feast of the universal church in 1264) it was not observed everywhere immediately and certain dioceses and religious orders adopted it only in the 14th century.

31. In a modern English translation, John Myrc's poem reads: No one in church should stand nor lean against pillar or wall, but fairly on their knees should they set themselves, kneeling on the floor. And pray to god with humble heart to give each of them grace and mercy. And when the gospel is over, teach them to kneel down immediately; and when they hear the bell ring for the holy sacring [consecration], teach them to kneel down, both young and old and to hold up both their hands and say then in this manner, fairly and softly, without hearing [silently]: "Jesus, Lo~ Welcome thou be, in form · bread as I thee see." John Myrc (or Mirc), *Instructions for Priests* (ca. 1400–50); Edward Peacock, ed., Early English Text Society 31 (London: Trübner, 1868), 9–11:

32. *The Poems of John Audelay,* E.K. Whiting, ed., Early English Text Society, Original Series 184 (London, 1931), 68.

33. See the so-called Cæremoniale of Gregory X, n. 19; M. Dykmans, ed., I: 208–209.

34. As mentioned in both Myrc's *Instruction for Parish Priests,* quoted in note 31 above, and in Audelay's *Poem no. 9,* quoted in the text above.

35. See J. Jungmann, MRR, II: 211; J. Kramp, "Messgebrauche der Gläubigen in den ausserdeutschen Ländern," *Stimmen der Zeit* 113 (1927/II), 352–367.

36. The canons of the Lateran had prostrated at this point on ferials since the 12th century.

37. Kneeling with bowed head became so common that by the beginning of the twentieth century scarcely any presumed to look up but instead bowed their heads at the elevation. In 1907, Pius X gave a new incentive to look at the host by granting an indulgence to those who, while contemplating the Host, said the prayer: "My Lord and my God"; J. Jungmann, MRR, II: 212.

38. The first evidence of the presiding minister kneeling before the consecrated species is a Franciscan decretal of 1359, but it takes place after the Lord's Prayer where all present recite Psalm 121. Later that same century we begin to find evidence of kneeling by the presider before the *Domine non sum dignus.*

39. Heinrich von Hesse, *Secreta Sacerdotum quae sibi placent vel displicent in missa* (Strasbourg, 1508), not paginated.

40. Ordo of Haymo of Haversham (1243): *Hoc est corpus meum. Et adorato corpore domini cum mediocri inclinatione elevet illud reverenter ita quod a circumstantibus possit videri. Postea deponit in loco suo;* S. J. P. Van Dijk, *Sources,* II: 11 (The full title of Haymo's order is *Incipit ordo agendorum et dicendorum a sacerdote in missa privata et feriali iuxta consuetudinem ecclesie romane.)* The Missal of the Curia (ca. 1270) still knows nothing of the elevation or accompanying genuflection: *Hoc est corpus meum. Hic reponat hostiam reverenter et levet calicem dicens* Simili. . . . [Rome, Vat. Ottob. lat 356, f. 114, J. Brinktrine, ed., *Ephemerides Liturgicae* 51 (1937): 204.], but see the *Ceremonial of the Cardinal-Bishop* by Latino Malabranca (ca. 1280): *[Pontifex] ipse primus adoret inclinato capite sacrum dominicum corpus; deinde reverenter et attente ipsum elevet in altum adorandum a populo et adoratam sacram hostiam deponat in loco suo. . . . In remissionem peccatorum. Quibus finitis inclinato paululum capite,*

adoret sacrum Domini sanguinem, et elevet adorandum a populo, ut supra de corpore dictum est. Nec oportet quod vel corpus vel calicem diu teneat elevatum sed post brevem horam deponat, ita tamen quod elevationes faciat cum debita reverentia et maturitate;" M. Dykmans, ed., *Le cérémonial papal,* I: 247–248.

41. Heinrich von Hesse, *Secreta Sacerdotum.*

42. According to the Ceremonial of Cardinals (ca. 1300) the assisting cardinal bishop *"In elevatione tamen dominici corporis poterit ad modicum flectere genua et idem similiter in elevatione calicis, adorando videlicet corpus et sanguinem consecratam."* M. Dykmans, ed., *Le cérémonial papal,* I: 270.

43. See J. Jungmann, MRR, II: 212-213. Bending one knee and rising immediately (the modern genuflection) was known in the thirteenth century as a mark of respect before the nobility. Berthold of Regensberg (†1272) stresses the distinction in one of his sermons and urges a "double" genuflection before the blessed sacrament; see Berthold von Regensburg, *Vollständige Ausgabe seiner deutschen Predigten,* F. Pfeiffer and J. Strobl, eds., (Vienna, 1862), I: 457.

44. *Hic adoret corpus Christi genibus flexis, deinde elevet . . . Hic adorat sanguinem et postea elevet dicens: 'Haec quotiescunque';* V. Leroquais, *Les Sacramentaires et les Missels manuscrits des bibliothèques publiques de France,* (Paris, 1924), III: 723.

45. R. Lippe, ed., *Misssale Romanum Mediolani 1474,* Henry Bradshaw Society 17 (London, 1899), I: 207.

46. *Missale Romanum Mediolani 1474,* Henry Bradshaw Society 33 (London, 1907), II: 110–111. The English Carthusians had around the year 1500 a semi-genuflection before the elevation but still no genuflection afterwards: *Ad 'Qui pridie quam pateretur' cum dicitur, accepit panem, accipit hostiam utraque manu et suo loco benedicit; dum dicit 'gratias agens' reverenter elevat oculos tenebitque hostiam ita in quantum potest quod a circumstantibus non videatur antequam elevatur. Consecrata hostia sacerdos antequam ipsam elevet parum geniculat; post elevationem deposita hostia reverenter inclinat sed non genuflectit.* [J. W. Legg, Tracts on the Mass, Henry Bradshaw Society 27 (London, 1904), 101]

47. J. Burchard, *Ordo servandus per Sacerdotem in celebratione Misse sine cantu et sine ministris secundum ritum sancte Romane ecclesie,* in J. W. Legg, Tracts on the Mass, 156-157.

48. The Sarum and Hereford Missals are good examples: The former, in its last edition (1557), makes no mention whatsoever of the genuflections at the words of institution; a bow is mentioned before the elevation of the host but not of the chalice; *Missale ad usum insignis et praeclare ecclesiae Sarum,* F. H. Dickenson, ed., (London, 1861–83 reprinted Farnborough: Gregg International, 1969), cols. 616–617; *Missale ad usum percele-bris ecclesiae Herefordensis,* W. G. Henderson, ed., (1874 reprinted Farnborough: Gregg International, 1969), 128–129.

49. See Pius V, *Quo Primum,* (14 July 1570).

50. See *AAS* 52 (1960): 683–85.

51. These choir rules would normally apply to all the faithful in attendance as well, but the actual practice varied greatly from country to country. At the time of Trent, for example, the Italians stood right after the consecration while the Portugese were used to kneeling "as long as the Lord's body was on the altar" i.e., until the priest's communion [H. Jedin, "Das Konzil von Trient und die Reform des Römisches Messbuches," *Liturgischen Leben* 6 (1939):30-36, here, 35.]; Aristocrats did not like to kneel at all since their clothing would be soiled and their long, turned-up shoes got in the way; [Adolph Franz, *Die Messe im Deutschen Mittlealter: Beiträge zur Geschichte der Liturgie und des religiösen Volkslebens* (Frieburg, 1902), 31, quoted in J. Jungmann, MRR, I: 242, n. 49].

52. Cf. *Missale Romanum. Rubricae Generales Missalis,* XVII–*De ordine genuflectendi, sedendi, et standi in Missa privata et solemni* (New York: Benziger, 1942), xxxi-xxxii.

53. *Ibid.,* 2: *Circumstantes autem in Missis privatis semper genua flectunt, etiam Tempore Paschali, præterquam dum legitur Evangelium,* (New York: Benziger, 1942), xxxi.

54. It is worth noting that even in this late period, the *"missa privata"* was not considered a

"*missa solitaria*" since the rubric explicitly mentions the *circumstantes*. On the origin of the private Mass see especially A. Häussling, *Mönchskonvent und Eucharistiefeier: Eine Studie über die Messe in der abendländischen Klosterliturgie des frühen Mittelalters und zur Geschichte der Messhäufigkeit*, Liturgiewissenschaftliche Quellen und Forschungen 58. (Münster, 1972) and the summary of current scholarship in W. G. Storey and J. Brooks-Leonard, revisors, "Excursus: The "Private Mass" in C. Vogel, *Medieval Liturgy* (Washington: Pastoral Press, 1986), 156–159.

55. *Missale Romanum; Ritus servandus in celebratione missae*, VI,8 (Benziger, 1942), xlvi.

56. See the excursus on the private Mass mentioned above in note 54.

57. J. Jungmann, MRR, I: 242.

58. Jungmann notes (MRR, I: 242–243, n. 49) that "at the request of many American bishops," J. O'Connell "included in his ceremonial rules for the laity that differ in little from the ordinary choir rules, and hence insist on a standing posture as basic;" cf. J. O'Connell, The *Celebration of Mass*, I: appendix.

59. Cf. R. Guardini, *Von heiligen Zeichen* (1922, Mainz 1926; 1946).

60. It was the intention of Trent to reform the missal *ad pristinam sanctorum Patrum normam ac ritum* (Pius V, *Quo Primum*, 14 July 1570). "Even if there had been further sources (than what was readily available in the Vatican Library),

one could not expect a commission composed of a few men and entrusted with a practical job, to anticipate in two years the liturgico-historical knowledge which would be attained only by the contiued efforts of many students during several centuries." J. Jungmann, MRR, I: 137.

61. Vatican II, *Constitution on the Sacred Liturgy* [SC] (December 4, 1963), nos. 21, 23; in ICEL, *Documents on the Liturgy 1963-1979: Conciliar, Papal, and Curial Texts* [DOL] (Collegeville: The Liturgical Press, 1982) [DOL 1, nos. 21, 23].

62. SC, no. 50; DOL 1:50.

63. "*Celebrans genuflectit tantum : a) cum accedit ad altare . . . , si adest tabernaculum cum Ss. Sacramento; b) post elevationem hostiae et post elevationem calicis; c) in fine Canonis post doxologiam* [later abolished in the altar Missal of 1970]; *d) ante communionem . . . ; e) expleta Communione, postquam hostias, quae forte superfuerint, in tabernaculo recondiderit. Reliquae genuflexiones omittuntur.* [The celebrant genuflects only: a) on going to . . . the altar if there is a tabernacle containing the blessed sacrament; b) after elevating the host and the chalice; c) after the doxology at the end of the canon [abolished in the Missal of 1970]; d) at communion . . . ; e) after the communion of the faithful, when he has placed the remaining hosts in the tabernacle. All other genuflections are omitted.]" (Sacred Congregation of Rites, *Tres abhinc annos*, Instruction on the orderly carrying out of the

Constitution on the Liturgy (May 4, 1967), n. 7; R. Kaczynski, *Enchiridion documentorum instaurationis liturgicae, I: 1963–1973* (Rome, 1976), n. 816; DOL 39, n. 453.

64. *"Tres genuflexiones fiunt in Missa, hoc est: post ostensionem Hostiae, post ostentionem calicis et ante Communionem.* [Three genuflections are made during Mass: after the showing of the eucharistic bread, after the showing of the chalice, and before communion.]" But "If there is a tabernacle with the blessed sacrament in the sanctuary, a genuflection is made before and after Mass and whenever anyone passes in front of the blessed sacrament. [*Si vero tabernaculum cum Ssmo. Sacramento sit in presbyterio, genuflecitur etiam ante et post Missam, et quoties quis ante Sacramentum transit.*] " Sacred Congregation for Divine Worship, *General Instruction of the Roman Missal* [GIRM] 4th ed., (March 27, 1975), n. 233; R. Kaczynski, n. 1628; DOL 208, n. 1623. Note well, the sacred species are to be shown to the people; at Masses where the priest faces the people, an elevation over the head is no longer warranted.

65. *"Ad ostentionem autem hostiam et calicem aspicientes ac postea profunde se inclinantes.* [They look at the eucharistic bread and chalice as these are shown and afterward bow low.]" GIRM, nos. 174c, 180c, 184c, 188c; R. Kaczynski, n. 1575; DOL 208, nos. 1564, 1570, 1574, 1578. Although the concelebrants may take the host from a paten passed among them, there is an indication in the GIRM that they may also approach the altar one by one and, after genuflecting, "take the body of Christ . . . and return to their places" They do the same thing if they are to receive communion by intinction. GIRM, nos. 197, 206; R. Kaczynski, nos. 1592, 1601; DOL 208, nos. 1587, 1596.

66. GIRM, n. 21; R. Kaczynski, n. 1416; DOL 208, no. 1411. NB. *Genuflectant* is the 3rd person plural present subjunctive of *genuflectere,* the same verb that is used to describe what the priest does at the consecration: *Celebrans genuflectit . . . post elevationem hostiae et post elevationem calicis* [The celebrant genuflects . . . after the elevation of the host and after the elevation of the chalice]."

67. Ibid.

68. Appendix to the General Instructions for the Dioceses of the United States of America, 21; Roman Missal, 1974, p. 45.

69. *"In super omnes, etiam Praelati, in choro genua flectunt: . . . c) in Missis feriarium Adventus, Quadragesimae et Passsionis, Quatuor Temporum mensis septembris, vigiliarum II et III classis extra tempus paschale, et in Missis defunctorum: ad orationes ante epistolam, dicto Dominus vobiscum; ab expleto Sanctus usque ad* Pater noster *cum sua praefatione exclusive; et ad orationes post Communionem et super populum.* [For the above, all those in the choir—even the bishop—kneel: . . . c) at weekday Masses during Advent, Lent and Passiontide, September ember days, 3rd and 4th class vigils outside Easter, and at Masses for the dead; for

the prayers before the reading from 'the Lord be with you'; from the Sanctus to the introduction to the 'Our Father'; and for the prayers after communion and the prayer over the people.]" *Acta Apostolica Sedis* 52 (1960):684.

70. Ibid. "*In super omnes, etiam Praelatis, in choro genua flectunt: a) ad Consecrationem.* [For the above, all these in the choir—even the bishop—kneel: a) at the consecration.]"

71. The authors are indebted to Ms. Elizabeth Hoffman of Liturgy Training Publications for the use of an unpublished term paper that includes a report on research she did in the archives of the NCCB and of the Bishops' Committee on the Liturgy in 1986. Copies of the documents she used were not available when requested from the Secretariat in 1992.

72. The point of departure for the reform should not be "private" Mass but "Mass with a congregation;" not Mass as read but Mass with singing. But which Mass with song—the pontifical, the solemn, or the simple sung Mass? Given the concrete situation in the churches, the answer can only be: Mass celebrated by a priest with a reader, servers, a choir or cantor, and a congregation. All other forms, such as pontifical Mass, solemn Mass, Mass with a deacon, will be amplifications or further simplifications of this basic Mass, which is there called "normative." Quoted from Annibale Bugnini, *The Reform of the Liturgy 1948–1975* (Collegeville: The Liturgical Press, 1990), 340.

73. Stephen Somerville of the Toronto Pastoral Centre for Liturgy picks apart the arguments of the Western Canadian *Reconsideration of Postures for the Laity at the Eucharist* in "Posture Perfect," *Fragments* 63 (December 1991):1–4. Andrew Beards fears that standing for the eucharistic prayer will lead to the complete abandonment of kneeling in "On Kneeling in the Liturgy," *Homiletic and Pastoral Review* 92:5 (February 1992):19–25. Peter M. J. Stravinskas considers the clamor for standing to be the "latest effort at desacralization" in *Rubrics of the Mass* (Huntington, IN: Our Sunday Visitor, 1992).

Bibliography

SOURCES

Amalarius of Metz. *Liber Officialis.* Latin text in J. M. Hanssens, ed., *Amalarii Episcopi Opera Liturgica Omnia.* 3 vols. Studi e Testi 138–140. Citta del Vaticano: Biblioteca Apostolica Vaticana, 1948.

Ambrose. *De Virginibus.* Latin text in PL 16: cols. 201, 205.

Apostolic Tradition of Hippolytus. English translation in Geoffrey J. Cuming, *Hippolytus: A Text for Students.* Grove Liturgical Study 8. Bramcote, Notts.: Grove Books, 1976.

Augustine of Hippo. *Ennarationes in Psalmos.* Latin text in *Corpus Christianorum.* Series Latina, [CCL], 38–40. Turnholt: Brepols, 1956.

_____. *Epistula 55 ad Januarium.* Latin text in *Corpus Scriptorum Ecclesiasticorum Latinorum* [CSEL], 34/2:202. Edited by the Vienna Academy. Vienna, 1866–present.

Bede the Venerable. *Homily II.* Latin text in *Corpus Christianorum.* Series Latina, 122: 298.

Bernhardi cardinalis et Lateranensis prioris Ordo officiorum ecclesiae Lateranensis. Edited by Ludwig Fischer. Historisches Forschungen und Quellen, 2/3. München und Friesing: F. P. Datterer, 1916.

Berthold of Regensberg. *Vollständige Ausgabe seiner deutschen Predigten.* Edited by F. Pfeiffer and J. Strobl. Vienna, 1862.

Burchard, John. *Ordo servandus per Sacerdotem in celebratione Misse sine cantu et sine ministris secundum ritum sancte Romane ecclesie.* In J. W. Legg, ed. *Tracts on the Mass.* Henry Bradshaw Society 27. London, 1904.

Ceremonial for Choir and Altar. In S.J.P. Van Dijk, *Sources of the Roman Liturgy.*

Ceremonial of Gregory X. In M. Dykmans, ed., *Le cérémonial papal de la fin du moyen âge a la renaissance.* Bibliotheque de l'Institut historique belge a Rome 24. Rome and Brussels, 1977.

Consuetudines Cluniacensis. Latin text in PL 149: cols. 715–25.

Documents on the Liturgy 1963–1979: Conciliar, Papal, and Curial Texts. [DOL]. Collegeville: The Liturgical Press, 1982.

Gregorian Sacramentary. See Deshusses, J. *Le Sacramentaire grégorian.* Spicilegium Friburgense 16. Fribourg, 1971.

Gregory of Tours. *Vitae Patrum.* Latin text in PL 71: col. 1093.

St. Jerome. *Contra Rufinam.* In P. Lardet, ed., *Saint Jérôme: Apologie contre Rufin.* Sources Chrétiennes 303. Paris: Editions du Cerf, 1983.

St. John Chrysostom. *Hom. XIV in Tim. 1:5.* Text in PG 62: col. 575.

Kaczynski, R., ed. *Enchiridion documentorum instaurationis liturgicae.* Rome, 1976.

Liber Sacramentorum Romanae Aeclesiae Ordinis Circuli. Edited by L. C. Mohlberg. Rerum Ecclesicasticarum Documenta. Series Major. Fontes IV. Rome: Herder, 1960.

Mansi, J. D., ed. *Sacrorum Conciliorum nova et amplissima collectio.* [Mansi]. 31 vols. Florence and Venice, 1757–1798. Paris, 1901–1927.

Migne, J.–P., ed. *Patrologiae cursus completus, Series Graeca.* [PG]. 161 vols. Paris, 1857–1866.

_____. *Patrologiae cursun completus, Series Latina.* [PL]. 221 vols. Paris, 1844–1864.

90

John Myrc's Instructions for Priests. Edited by Edward Peacock. Early English Text Society 31. London: Trübner, 1868.

Missale ad usum insignis et praeclare ecclesiae Sarum. Edited by F. H. Dickinson. London, 1861–83; reprinted Farnborough: Gregg International, 1969.

Missale ad usum percelebris ecclesiae Herefordensis. Edited by W. G. Henderson. London, 1874; reprinted Farnborough: Gregg International, 1969.

Missale Romanum. New York: Benziger, 1942.

Missale Romanum. Editio Typica. Typis Polyglottis Vaticanis, 1971.

Missale Romanum Mediolani 1474. Edited by Robert Lippe. Henry Bradshaw Society 17. London, 1899.

Les Ordines Romani de haut moyen âge. Edited by M. Andrieu. 5 vols. Spicilegium Sacram Lovaniense 11, 23, 24, 28, 29. Louvain, 1931–1961.

Ordo of Haymo of Haversham. In S. J. P. Van Dijk, *Sources of the Roman Liturgy: Leiden: Frill, 1963.*

Origen. *Peri Euche (De Oratione)* ch. 31,2; in P. Koetschau, *Die Griechischen Christlichen Schriftsteller der ersten drei Jahrhunderte* (Berlin: Akademie Verlag, 1899), III:267.

Plato. *Laws.* Greek text found in G. Stallbaum, ed., *Platonis Opera Omnia.* Vol X: *Leges et Epinomis.* New York: Garland, 1980. English translation found in T. Pangle, *The Laws of Plato.* New York: Basic Books, 1980.

Pliny the Elder. *Historia naturalis.* In A. Ernout, ed. *Pline l'Ancien. Histoire Naturelle.* Paris: Société d'Édition "Les Belles Letters," 1962.

The Poems of John Audelay. Edited by E. K. Whiting. Early English Text Society, Ordinal Series 184. London, 1931.

Le Pontifical romain au Moyen-Âge. Edited by M. Andrieu. 4 vols. Studi e Testi 86–88, 99. Citta del Vaticano: Biblioteca Apostolica Vaticana, 1938–41.

Le Pontifical romano-germanique de dixième siècle. Edited by C. Vogel. 2 vols. Studi e Testi 226–227. Citta del Vaticano: Biblioteca Apostolica Vaticana, 1963.

Ps-Justin. *Quaestiones ad orthodoxos.* Text in PG 6: col. 1363.

Sacramentarium Veronense. Edited by Leo. C. Mohlberg, et al. Rerum Ecclesiasticarum Documenta, Series Major. Fontes I. Rome: Herder, 1956.

General Instruction of the Roman Missal (1975). [GIRM]. In *Documents on the Liturgy 1963–1979.*

Tres abhinc annos (Instruction on the orderly carrying out of the Constitution on the Liturgy) (1967). In *Documents on the Liturgy 1963–1979.*

Tertullian. *Apology;* PL 1:503–504; CCL 1:141–142.

_____. *De Oratione liber.* Latin text and translation in Ernest Evans, ed. *Tertullian's Tract on Prayer.* London: SPCK, 1953.

_____. *De Resurrectione Mortuorum.* Latin text in *Corpus Christianorum.* Series Latina, II: 931. Trans. in Palmer, Paul. *Sacraments and Worship.* London: Darton, Longman & Todd, 1957.

Sacrosanctum Concilium (Constitution on the Sacred Liturgy) (1963). [SC] English translation in *Documents on the Liturgy 1963–1979.*

BOOKS AND ARTICLES

Baldovin, John F. *The Ubran Character of Christian Worship in Jerusalem, Rome, and Constantinople.* Orientalia Christiana Analecta 228. Rome, 1987.

Beards, Andrew. "On Kneeling in the Liturgy." *Homiletic and Pastoral Review* 92 (February 1992): 19–25.

Bright, William, *Canons of the First Four Councils of Nicea, Constantinople, Ephesus and Chalcedon,* 2nd ed. (Oxford: Clarendon Press, 1892).

Browe, P. *"L'affiamento del corpo durante la messa."* *Ephemerides Liturgicae* 50 (1936): 402–14.

Bugnini, Annibale. *The Reform of the Liturgy 1948–1975.* Collegeville: The Liturgical Press, 1990.

Chavasse, A. *Le Sacramentaire gélasien* (Vat. Reg., 316). Paris, 1958.

Crawley, A. E. "Kissing." In Hastings, James, ed. *Encyclopedia of Religions and Ethics.* New York: Scribners, 1955.

Delatte, A. "Le baiser, l'agenouillement el le prosternement de l'adoration (proskýnēsis) chez les Grecs." *Bullet de la Classe de Lettres et des Sciences Morales et Politiques.* Académie royale de Belgique 37 (1951): 423–44.

de Lenval, Helene Lubienska. *The Whole Man at Worship: The Actions of Man before God.* Translated by Rachel Attwater. New York: Desclee Company, 1961.

Dictionnaire d'árcheologie chrétienne it de liturgie. Edited by F. Cabrol, H. Leclercq, and H. Marrou. 15 vols. Paris, 1907–1973.

Douglas, M. "Deciphering a Meal." *Daedalus* 101 (1972).

Dumoutet, E. *Le Désir de Voir l'Hostie.* Paris: Beauchesne, 1926.

Ebner, A. *Quellen und Forschungen zur Geschichte und Kunstgeschichte des Missale Romanum im Mitterlalter.* Freiburg, 1896.

Encyclopedia of Theology. Edited by K. Rahner. New York: Seabury, 1975.

Guardini, R. *Von heiligen Seichen.* Mainz, 1926, 1946.

Hefele, Charles J., and Leclercq, Henri. *Histoire des Conciles.* 11 vols. Paris: Letouzey et Ane, 1907–1952.

Heiler, Frederich. *Das Gebt: Eine religionsgeschichtliche und religionspsychologische Untersuchungen.* 4th ed. Munich, 1923. See McComb, S., tr. and ed. *Prayer: A Study in the History and Psychology of Religion.* New York: Oxford University Press, 1958.

Jal, P., ed. *Tite-Live. Histoire Romaine*, Livre XLV. Paris: Sociétè d'Édition "Les Belles Letters," 1979.

Jedin, H. "*Das Konzil von Trient und die Reform des Römisches Messbuches.*" *Liturgischen Leben* 6 (1939): 30–36.

Jungmann, Josef A. *The Mass of the Roman Rite.* [MRR]. 2 vols. New York: Benziger, 1955; reprint Westminister, 1986.

_____. *"Flectere pro Carole rege." Mélanges Andrieu.* Strasbourg, 1956.

Kennedy, V. L. "The Moment of Consecration and the Elevation of the Host." *Mediaeval Studies* 6 (1944): 122–50.

_____. "The Date of the Parisian Decree on the Elevation of the Host." *Mediaeval Studies* 8 (1946): 87–96.

Kramp, J. "Messegebrauche der Gläubigen in den ausserdeutschen Ländern." *Stimmen der Zeit* 113 (1927): II, 352–67.

Legg, J. W., ed. *Tracts on the Mass.* Henry Bradshaw Society 27. London, 1904.

Léroquais, Victor. *Les Sacramentaires et les Missels manuscrits des biblotèques publiques de France.* Paris, 1924.

Marti, Berthe M. *"Proskynesis* and *Adorare." Language* 12 (1936): 272–82.

Mitchell, Nathan. *Cult and Controversy: The Worship of the Eucharist Outside Mass.* New York: Pueblo, 1982.

Neunheuser, Burkhard. *"Les Gestes de la Prière à genoux et de la génuflexion dans les églises de rite romain,"* in A. M. Triacca, et. al., eds., *Gestes et Paroles,* 153.

Rahner, K. and Vorgrimler, H. *Theological Dictionary.* Edited by C. Ernst, translated by R. Strachan. New York: Herder & Herder, 1965.

Reeves, W. *The Culdees of the British Islands.* Dublin, 1864.

Smith, Dennis and Taussig, Hal. *Many Tables: The Eucharist in the New Testament and Liturgy Today.* Philadelphia: Trinity Press International, 1990.

Somerville, Stephen. "Posture Perfect." *Fragments* 63 (December 1991): 1–4.

Stevenson, J., ed. *A New Eusebius.* London: SPCK, 1968.

Stravinskas, M. J. *Rubrics of the Mass.* Huntington, IN: Our Sunday Visitor, 1992.

Suntrup, Rudolf. *Die Bedeutung der liturgischen Gebärden und Bewegungen in lateinischen und deutschen Auslegungen des 9. bis 13. Jahrhunderts.* Münstersche Mitterlalter Schriften, 37. München: Wilhelm Fink Verlag, 1978.

Taft, Robert. *Beyond East and West.* Washington, DC: Pastoral Press, 1984.

_____. *The Liturgy of the Hours in East and West.* Collegeville: The Liturgical Press, 1986.

Tirot, Paul. "Un *Ordo Missae* monastique: Cluny, Citeaux, la Chartreuse," *Ephemerides Liturgicae* 95 (1981): 44–120; 220–51.

Triacca, A. M. et. al., eds. *Gestes et Paroles dans les diverses Familles liturgiques.* Conférences Saint–Serge XXIVe Semaine d'etudes liturgiques, Paris, 28e Juin–1er Juillet 1977. Biblioteca Ephermerides Liturgicae Subsidia 14. Rome: Centro Liturgico Vincenziane, 1978.

Van Dijk, S. J. P. *Sources of the Roman Liturgy.* Leiden: Brill, 1963.

Vogel, C. *Medieval Liturgy: An Introduction to the Sources.* Revised and translated by W. Storey and N. Rasmussen with the assistance of J. Brooks-Leonard. Washington, DC: Pastoral Press, 1986.

von Hesse, Heinrich. *Secreta Sacerdotum quae sibi placent vel displicent in missa.* Strasbourg, 1508.

Suggested resources on the eucharist from Liturgy Training Publications:

Dallen, James. *The Dilemma of Priestless Sundays* (1994).

Huck, Gabe. *The Communion Rite at Sunday Mass* (1989).

La Verdiere, Eugenc. *Dining in the Kingdom of God: The Origins of the Eucharist According to Luke* (1994).

Mitchell, Nathan. *Eucharist as Sacrament of Initiation.* Forum Essays, No. 2 (1994).

Lift Up Your Hearts: The Eucharistic Prayer. 30 minute video (1994).

Say Amen! to What You Are. 30 minute video (1994).